The Earth and Its Mountains

Folds in the vicinity of Borah Peak (or 'Mt. Borah' on some maps) N of Mackay, Idaho Looking ca. NW

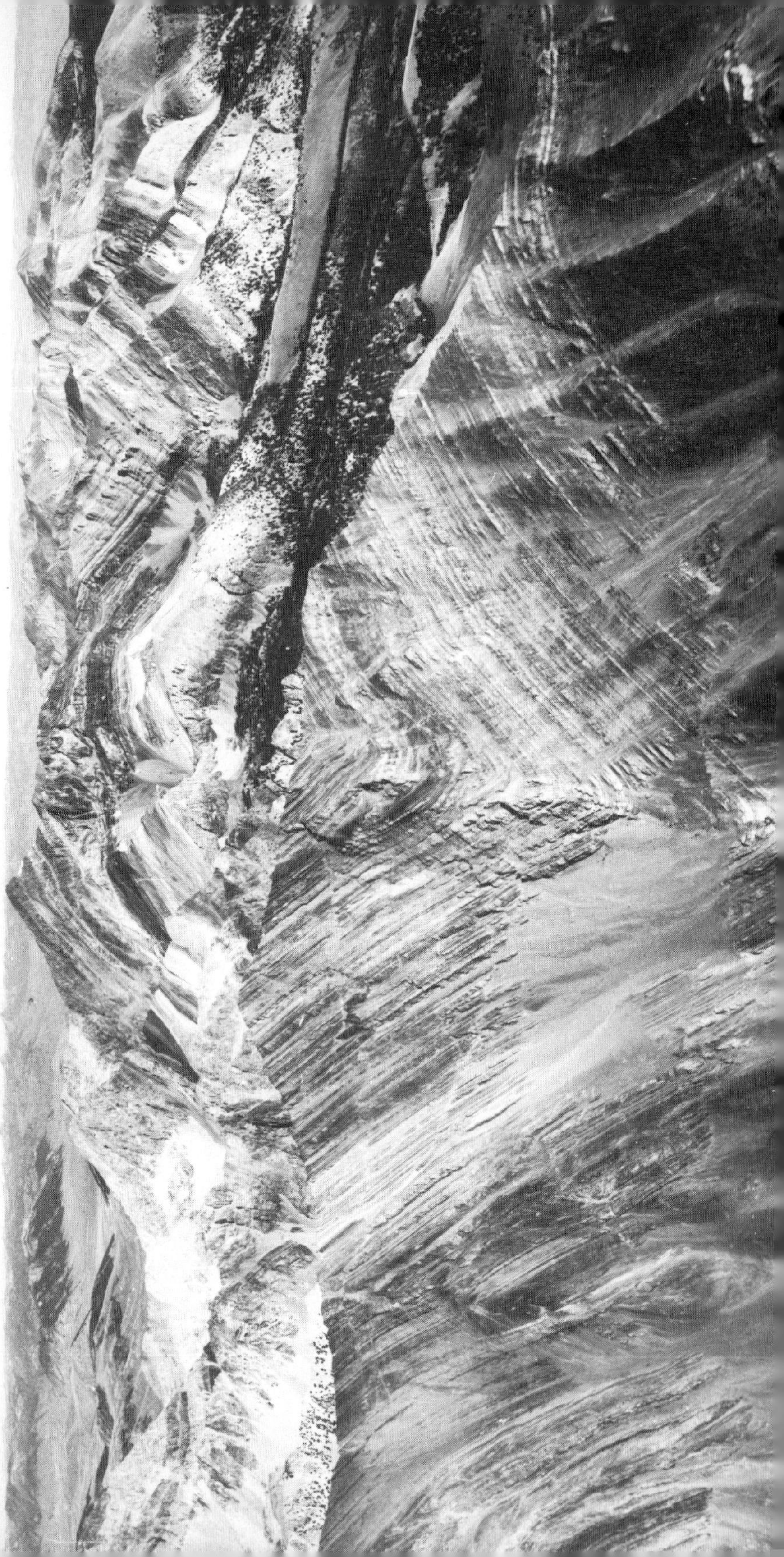

The Earth and Its Mountains

R. A. Lyttleton F.R.S.

Formerly Professor of Theoretical Astronomy
University of Cambridge

A Wiley–Interscience Publication

175 YEARS OF PUBLISHING
1807 1982

JOHN WILEY & SONS
Chichester · New York · Brisbane · Toronto · Singapore

British Library Cataloguing in Publication Data:

Lyttleton, R.A.
The earth and its mountains.
1. Earth sciences
I. Title
551.1 QE26.2

ISBN 0 471 10530 9

Printed in Great Britain

Contents

Preface

In 1978 the Milne Society honoured me by an invitation to deliver the annual Milne Lecture under the auspices of Wadham College and the Mathematical Institute of Oxford University. The title adopted for the Lecture was Gravitation, Ancient Eclipses, and Mountains.

The occasion provided an opportunity to give a coherent account of ideas on the theory of the structure of the Earth that had been under investigation by the author during the past two decades, and the present book covers more fully topics that could only be dealt with briefly in a single lecture to a general audience. In certain respects these new ideas differ widely from views that have long since come to be regarded as being established beyond reasonable doubt. The views here put forward lead in the first place to the conclusion that the Earth (and other terrestrial planets) began their individual existences in solid form throughout, and that the basic cause of their evolution is the still-continuing release of energy in their interiors by the long-life radioactive elements uranium, thorium, and potassium.

The central novel feature that this book offers for consideration concerns the age-old standard theory of tidal friction of the Earth-Moon-Sun system, which for over forty years has been generally accepted without question as correct. However, with improved values of the apparent secular accelerations of the Moon and Sun becoming available in the early 1970s, a re-working of the tidal-friction theory disclosed that an invalid dynamical assumption had tacitly been made in setting up the fundamental initial equations of the theory. This error has passed unnoticed by geophysicists for several decades despite its frequent re-publication during this period. It turns out that correction of the error has far-reaching and profound consequences for geophysics as a whole, particularly in showing that the moment-of-inertia of the Earth is steadily decreasing, and with it on average also the surface-radius. The existing seismic data show that when originally in all-solid form, the moment-of-inertia of the Earth would have been over 25% greater than at present, with the radius some 370 km greater, and the amended theory also shows that the long-standing assumption that the core consists of iron and nickel cannot be sustained. But perhaps the conclusion of most general interest that emerges from the revised theory is that contraction of the Earth sufficient to account for more than twenty major eras of mountain-building must have taken place, a scale of contraction that geologists have considered essential from time immemorial.

These conclusions importantly affect many areas of geophysics, and in order that a reader may more easily appreciate the general account of the formation and evolution of the Earth, the book commences with brief, non-technical summaries of each chapter, before the full mathematical exposition which comprises the main body of the work is given.

The book is not intended as a comprehensive textbook on geophysics, which would need an encyclopaedic volume. Nor, it should be emphasised, does it attempt to deal with the purely verbal and pictorial explanations of alleged terrestrial phenomena now in vogue, not because these already have been widely disseminated in a vast and repetitive literature, but because in the author's view they simply do not constitute scientific theories in the proper sense at all.

My special acknowledgments of his assistance are due to Professor J.P. Fitch, now of the University of Bath, who carried out an immense number of computations of the properties of terrestrial and planetary models (not included in this book) in order to make certain that the results put forward herein were independent overall of any particular assumptions and approximations relied upon. Though based on work over many years, the book itself was written mainly in 1979 when the author was holder of a Leverhulme Fellowship, and my grateful thanks are therefore due to the Leverhulme Trustees for the benefit that their award contributed to numerous aspects of the book.

November 1981 R. A. LYTTLETON

Chapter Summaries

1 - THE ORIGIN OF THE EARTH 1 - 25

The famous nebular hypothesis of Laplace regarded all the planets as being initially gaseous. The theory provided no origin for the nebula itself, and the ultimate central body to which the nebula contracted, and to be identified with the Sun, would have far too rapid rotation. Replacement of the theory by tidal or collisional encounters of the Sun with a passing star also implied initially gaseous planets, and also failed by a large factor to account for the enormous scale of the planetary orbits in comparison with the size of the Sun. However, if otherwise acceptable, these theories could be saved by supposing that the Sun originally possessed a companion-star already moving at distances from it of the required planetary order, and it would be from this body and the passing star that the necessary planetary material would be released in a close encounter. In addition as a result of the encounter, the companion-star would have its motion speeded up sufficiently to overcome its weak gravitational binding to the Sun and cause it to escape. Or again, if the companion were sufficiently massive to reach a supernova explosion stage, the Sun could capture a mere wisp of the material thereby ejected into space, and the slightest asymmetry of recoil could release the remnant star from its binding to the Sun. The captured material would expand and cool to form a pre-planetary nebular disc rotating round the Sun, and this would subsequently develop into a set of planets. Such a nebula of suitable mass and adequate range of extension from the Sun could also readily be captured from an interstellar gas-and-dust cloud, which abound within the Galaxy. This could occur directly by accretion by the Sun, or through the combined dynamical action involving another adjacent star. Such occurrences may happen so often in the Galaxy that a great many stars may at some time have captured a nebular gas-and-dust disc in this way, and come to possess a retinue of planets. The dust component would necessarily settle into a flat disc only a few centimetres thick, with all its elements in circular orbital motion round the Sun, and the density in this disc would be high enough for planets to aggregate by gravitational forces. But due to the thinness of the disc, the material gathered into a growing planet would fall only onto a narrow circumferential band, and no general heating of the whole surface would take place. The Earth would take about 50,000 years to reach its present mass. The Moon would have been an embryo planet adjacent to the Earth in its orbit, first captured by the Earth and then becoming permanently bound to it as a result of only slight further infall of the last vestiges of the dust disc. Planets so formed would have rotation periods of a few hours resulting from the vorticity inherent in the disc-material through its orbital motion about the Sun, but subsequent tidal actions would slow the rotations. This mechanism of formation shows that the Earth and other terrestrial planets and the Moon can never have been wholly gaseous or molten but began their individual existences sufficiently cool to be solid throughout their entire volumes.

Radioactive elements of long half-lives, comparable with the age of the Earth itself, such as uranium, thorium, and potassium would gradually raise the internal temperature of the Earth and must still be continuing to do so especially in the deep interior. There is a peculiarly high concentration of these elements in the extreme outer layers, but this concentration cannot possibly continue on downwards or the Earth would be at such a high temperature as to be molten throughout. This curious feature could have resulted from a subsequent slight addition of interstellar material of high radioactive content, but this property is not of great importance to the general evolution of the Earth. There is some evidence of a similar high concentration of these radioactive elements in the lunar surface-layers.

These particular radioactive elements enable the ages of rocks that contain them to be ascertained. Estimates of the age of the Earth so arrived at have gradually crept up during the last half-century, and the figure has presently reached about 4,500,000,000 years, but even if greater estimates emerge, certain theoretical considerations show that the age is unlikely to be as great as 6,000,000,000 years.

Seismic data inferred from the travel-times of earthquake-waves reveal the physical properties at all depths within the Earth, but not the actual chemical composition of the material. Analysis of the data indicates the presence of several successive concentric spherical layers at which reflections and refractions of waves occur. For broader questions, these layers can be merged into three main zones : first, an outer shell extending to a depth of 413 km ; then below that the solid mantle to depth 3898 km ; and next, a liquid core of radius 3473 km containing over 31 per cent of the whole mass. There is some evidence that a solid core of small mass and radius may exist at the very centre within the liquid core. The seismic data lead to the highly important conclusion that the core-material in its metallic liquid phase is much more compressible than the mantle-material in the solid phase. Also the uncompressed density of the core-material is far too low for identification with iron and nickel in any proportions, a result first established by W.H. Ramsey some thirty or more years ago.

Over long periods of time, the angular velocity of the Earth and the orbital motion of the Moon are importantly affected by the phenomenon of tidal friction. It results from the tides raised by the differential gravitational action of the Moon and Sun upon the Earth owing to the finite size and non-rigidity of the latter. These tides occur in the oceans and seas, in the atmosphere, and also in the solid body of the Earth. Because of the more rapid rotation of the Earth as compared with the orbital angular rates of the Moon and Sun about it, such tides mainly lag behind the bodies producing them, and this results in forces that dissipate the energy of rotation of the Earth. But the total rotatory momentum of the Earth-Moon system cannot be changed by internal forces, and that lost by the Earth is transferred to the lunar orbit causing the Moon to recede slowly. The amount of tidal dissipation presently occurring is extremely difficult to calculate directly, and more so for past times when conditions may have been much different from now. However, the data provided by ancient-eclipse records, which extend back about 3000 years, enable the rate of change of the rotation of the Earth, the rate of recession of the Moon, and the rate of change of the moment-of-inertia of the Earth to be calculated by means of trustworthy dynamical theory. The actual tracks on the surface of the Earth by the lunar shadow during an ancient-eclipse have been found to be far remote from the theoretical tracks calculated on the basis of purely conservative gravitational forces, and the differences reveal that the rotation of the Earth and the motion of the Moon are sensibly influenced by tidal friction. That the Moon appears to have a deceleration in its angular velocity round the Earth was first announced by Halley, and the problem was later studied by Euler, Laplace, and J.C. Adams. But it was Adams who finally established beyond any question that the Moon was undergoing an acceleration (negative) of its longitude inexplicable dynamically, since the observed longitude exhibits a minute term depending on the square of the time. This anomalous term produces a displacement of the position of the Moon that amounts to about half a degree, about its own diameter, in a thousand years. The rotation of the Earth has also been proved to be influenced by the same dissipative forces, and as a result its use as a true measure of dynamical time has had to be abandoned. In recent years, it has been replaced by so-called ephemeris-time depending on the motion of the Earth about the Sun, and in addition by atomic time defined by means of the cycles of a caesium-resonator.

Since both the rotation of the Earth and the angular velocity of the Moon in its orbit are undergoing accelerations, the ancient-eclipse data cannot lead to the values of these directly, but only to the combination of their effects, the so-called apparent secular accelerations of the Moon and Sun. These are related by certain strict dynamical equations to the lunar and solar couples. Hitherto, in setting up these equations, it has always been tacitly assumed that the moment-of-inertia of the Earth about its axis was an invariable constant not changing with time, but even so, had a proper solution of these dynamical equations ever been carried out, it would have led to the entirely unacceptable result that the total solar couple was acting to speed up the rotation of the Earth, and hence that the theory was in some way in error. The correct form of the equations of motion yield the lunar couple directly irrespective of whether any other complications may be involved in the problem, such as the changing moment-of-inertia, and even if the constant of gravitation were changing with time. The lunar couple turns out to be of such magnitude and form as to imply that the Moon would have been almost in contact with the Earth only about 1,000,000,000 years ago, and suggesting that other influences must have been involved over and above those yet recognised. The solar couple can then be found from the lunar couple by dimensional scaling, according to the type of tidal friction involved, but whatever basis is adopted for this latter, the results show inescapably that the moment-of-inertia is decreasing at a rate of essential importance in the whole problem. This in turn produces an intrinsic accelerative component in the angular velocity, as if an apparent or fictitious couple were acting on the Earth in order to conserve the rotatory momentum. On the other hand, the lunar and solar couples operate to retard the terrestrial rotation. The deceleration caused by the Moon is greater in magnitude than the intrinsic acceleration owing to the decreasing moment-of-inertia, and this in turn is greater in magnitude than the deceleration produced by the Sun. Thus the term hitherto overlooked in the theory is intermediate in magnitude between the lunar and solar couples, and its inclusion absolutely essential to acceptable dynamical interpretation of the ancient-eclipse data, which themselves are not in question as to their reliability. Not only does the conclusion that the moment-of-inertia is decreasing with time follow inescapably, but the further conclusion that the Earth as a whole is undergoing contraction.

5 - THE PHASE-CHANGE HYPOTHESIS 85 - 110

The physical cause of this contraction depends on what is termed a change of phase of the solid mantle material to liquid metallic form. With steadily rising internal temperature through radioactive energy-release and at the pressures prevailing in the central regions, a phase-change of solid mantle-material to a liquid metallic phase is continuously occurring at the mantle-core boundary. The belief that the core consists of iron and nickel, which down the years has come to be widely accepted has no serious validity, and all along has been based on arguments that can now be seen to be of nugatory value. W.H.Ramsey was the first to show theoretically that at pressures of the order of a million atmospheres and temperatures of a few thousand degrees such a phase-change would take place when either the pressure or the temperature exceeded certain critical values. Static pressures and temperatures of these orders are now coming within experimental producibility in the laboratory, and numerous phase-changes have already been shown to occur. The seismic data show the mantle-core transition to be extremely sharp, not at all to be expected for a compositional change, and this receives explanation on the phase-change theory, as also do certain curious properties of the primary and secondary wave-velocities as the innermost boundary of the mantle is approached from above.

The density-increase from solid to liquid form consequent on the phase-change is by a factor greater than 1.5, and this implies theoretically that when conditions suitable for the phase-change are reached with rising central temperature a sudden collapse of the Earth will have occurred with the formation in a matter of minutes of a liquid metallic core of initial radius 2,040 km, while the outer surface-radius undergoes an accompanying sudden decrease by 70 km. Thereafter, as the temperature at the mantle-core boundary continues to rise, the Earth evolves steadily through stable configurations, the mass and radius of the liquid core steadily increase, but the Earth as a whole undergoes contraction.

With increasing depth from the surface, the melting point temperature increases, but for the high-pressure liquid-core phase the density is greater than that of the solid-mantle phase, and as a thermodynamic consequence melting would start at the centre where the pressure is greatest in an all-solid Earth. Ramsey showed that at pressures of the order of a million atmospheres the incompressibility would be a closely linear function of the pressure, and from this could be inferred that the core-material would have uncompressed density of only 4.8 g/cm^3, rendering any identification with iron or nickel impossible.

The seismic data enable the physical properties of the Earth to be inferred at all depths, and a relation between pressure and density emerges for each of the three main zones. The relation is practically linear and independent of temperature. By use of these data, computer-techniques enable evolutionary models of an Earth of increasing liquid core-mass to be calculated in detail. In both 3-zone and 2-zone models, the conditions and properties in each zone can be determined by solution of a second-order differential equation which happens to be of Emden-form. The boundary conditions to be satisfied by a physically possible model-solution are that the density must be finite at the centre, and that the pressure must vanish at the precise radial distance at which the total mass encompassed within that distance is equal to the mass of the planet. For each member of a series of adopted values of the core-mass, such calculations yield the surface-radius, the moment-of-inertia, and the total gravitational energy, together with the general march of values from the centre to the surface of the pressure, density, and other associated quantities.

As the core-mass increases from zero, the pressure at the boundary between the liquid core and the solid mantle at first increases, strengthening the conditions there for a change of phase to proceed outwards. Thus the zone of phase-change to liquid form extends rapidly at first, and it is in this way that the Ramsey-collapse manifests itself when evolution is followed by means of static models. This interface-pressure increases to a maximum with increasing core-mass but thereafter always decreases monotonically. After the sudden collapse and initial formation of a large core in liquid metallic form, all quantities continue to change only steadily and uniformly with rising temperature, and the Earth evolves steadily through thoroughly stable forms. Both the moment-of-inertia and the calculated surface-radius steadily diminish. The results for 2-

zone models with increasing liquid-core mass surrounded by solid mantle-material follow an exactly similar course. The Earth may have remained in all-solid form for a time of the order of a billion years before the central temperature had risen sufficiently for the onset of the collapse, but the average rate of decrease of the moment-of-inertia is only weakly dependent on the adopted time of collapse. The accompanying intrinsic component of acceleration of rotation agrees closely with that determined from the ancient-eclipse data.

Among the terrestrial planets, only in the Earth and Venus are pressures high enough for the Ramsey phase-change. The associated density-jumps are both considerably greater than 1.5, and thus when the central temperature had risen to the critical value sudden collapse will have occurred. Before this temperature has been reached, ordinary melting may have taken place in a layer within a few hundred kilometres of the surface, and within it denser material would sink and lighter material rise. When later the collapse occurs of the whole Earth, with a sudden reduction of the outer radius by 70 km, the solid shell above this liquefied layer would be forced to undergo intense fracturing during the enormous reduction of surface-area. From such fissures the low-density underlying molten matter would well up to the surface under hydrostatic forces, and could thereby give rise to the less-dense continental material. Of the total gravitational energy released in the collapse, more than three-quarters goes to doing work on the material that becomes the metallic liquid core, and is about twice that actually needed solely for the phase-change. The rest of the energy goes to increasing the rotation-rate of the planet and to the necessary compression of the material remaining in solid form.

After the collapse, the Earth is thoroughly stable but evolves with further rising internal temperature, and contracts steadily everywhere, since the pressures far exceed the strength of the material, except in the extreme outer layers. In these, stresses gradually increase as a result of diminishing support from below, and must eventually become great enough to overcome their strength. Folding and thrusting must then occur at the weakest places and result in the formation of mountains. The most violent epoch of mountain-building would of course have been the few minutes of the initial collapse itself. The subsequent decrease of radius has been about 300 km so far, and thus averages about 0.01 cm per year. This means a total decrease of surface-area by nearly 50 million square kilometres, and a total volume of solid material of more than 150 billion cubic kilometres somehow to be redistributed at the surface. If shared out for say at least twenty eras of mountain-building at intervals of order 100,000,000 years, this would involve 8 billion cubic kilometres of solid material being redistributed by folding and thrusting during each epoch, enough to provide for some 200 mountain ranges of volume comparable with the Rocky Mountains, for example.

Between the successive comparatively short periods of mountain-building, continually rising temperature at the level of the Bernal-discontinuity would cause slight expansion of the Earth and rifting of the outer layers at their tensionally weakest places would occur, but the amount of this expansion would be far outweighed by the contraction resulting from the steady increase of the liquid-core mass. If the phase-change process is the true cause of mountain-building, it would make clear why all hitherto proposed mechanisms have proved to be inadequate and unacceptable.

When radioactive energy-release eventually becomes negligible, some 10^{11} to 10^{12} years hence, the interior of the Earth will begin to cool down, and the stages of the phase-change will proceed in the opposite direction. The liquid core will decrease in mass and radius and the Earth will expand, steadily and gradually at first, but then at a certain stage the whole of the remaining liquid-core will suddenly revert to mantle-form, accompanied by an explosive expansion of the whole Earth, the outer radius increasing in a matter of minutes by several tens of kilometres.

On the hypothesis of their all having the same composition, only in Venus of the other terrestrial planets would the central pressure be high enough for the phase-change conditions to be reached and lead to production of a liquid core. Now that the solid radius of Venus is known, a satisfactory 3-zone model can be calculated with properties similar to those of Earth, which indicates slightly higher internal temperatures at corresponding depths. The liquid core at present contains 25 per cent of the total mass and has radius 3032 km, while the Bernal-discontinuity is at a depth of 515 km. The general evolution of Venus will have been similar to that of the Earth, though the initial collapse would have been delayed till higher central temperature was reached to offset the lower central pressure. When at first in all-solid form, the surface-radius would have been 6306 km. The initial liquid-core contained 4.5 per cent of the total mass, and had radius 1750 km. The sudden collapse would have reduced the outer radius by 45 km, and since then, internal contraction has led to a further decrease of 206 km to the present value. Mountain-building by folding and thrusting will therefore occur at intervals on Venus, and recent radar-measures are already finding large-scale irregularities with differences of elevation as great as 10 km.

For Mars, pressures are sufficient only for the Bernal phase-change, and thus the planet will be a 2-zone all-solid body of mantle-material surrounded by outer-shell type material. The measured radius indicates lower internal temperatures than at equal depths in the Earth, and the discontinuity occurs at a depth of about 560 km. As no metallic-liquid core will have formed, there can be no dipole magnetic field, nor any folded and thrusted mountains. Since the Bernal discontinuity requires higher pressures as the temperature rises, its level must get progressively deeper, and the planet expand to produce rifting of the surface-layers. All these predictions were subsequently verified by means of the Mariner-missions to the planet.

In the Moon, the central pressure is far too low even for the Bernal phase-change. It is thus a 1-zone body of material of the same form as the outer-shell of the Earth. Although the outer surface shows irregularities on almost every scale produced by bombardment, in the absence of any phase-change core there can be no dipole magnetic field, and no folded and thrusted mountains, nor even rifting of the surface-layers. Compression decreases the radius by less than 10 km, and the calculated value is 0.7 km less than the observed radius, a deficiency readily explicable through non-hydrostatic conditions in the near-surface layers.

The mass and radius of Mercury, generally accepted for a great many years, imply the extraordinarily high mean-density of 5.43 g/cm^3, which would require the planet to contain over 60 per cent by mass of iron. On any basis as to its internal structure, the central pressure is sufficient only for the Bernal phase-change, which means that no folded and thrusted mountains would be formed, and this was confirmed by recent fly-pasts. Despite the seemingly very different composition from the other terrestrial planets, Mercury does not supply any test relevant to the Ramsey phase-change theory, since the internal pressures are far too low. The mass which is currently accepted dates back to Newcomb (1895) but it has only recently come to light that the value that he announced may have been in error as not really being supported by his calculations. However, Mercury is so near the Sun and of such small mass anyway that such error could well not have obtruded itself in observations not specifically aimed at detecting it, such as the placing of a satellite in orbit about the planet.

9 - IS THE CONSTANT OF GRAVITATION CONSTANT ? 177 - 193

In recent years new cosmological theories have been proposed that raise the question whether the constant of gravitation G is an absolute physical constant not changing with time, as the general-relativity theory requires it to be. If G were <u>decreasing</u> with time, as most of the theories suggest, the principal direct effect would be a purely kinematic <u>increase</u> with time of the linear dimensions of all orbits in the solar system, including the lunar orbit ; and conversely if G were increasing with time. When this possibility is allowed for, additional terms enter the equations of the theory of tidal friction, but the revised forms for the apparent secular accelerations of the Moon and Sun again are such that the lunar tidal couple N can be uniquely solved for, and it emerges unchanged in value. But the term $N' + \dot{C}\omega$ now becomes replaced by the sum $N' + \dot{C}\omega + 2C\omega\dot{G}/G$, and as before additional considerations are needed for the individual values of the three terms to be found. The value of $\dot{G}/G$ depends simply on the particular cosmology adopted, but if $\dot{G}$ is non-vanishing the ordinary forces of gravity within the Earth would be changing, obviously being stronger in the past if $\dot{G}$ is negative, and this must be allowed for in computing Earth-models with a view to finding $\dot{C}$. If $\dot{G}/G = -3 \times 10^{-11}$/yr, for example, the resulting calculated values of $\dot{\omega}_i/\omega$ show only weak agreement with the values derived from tidal-friction theory. However, substantial contraction of the Earth nevertheless is found to occur, the effects of the phase-change process still dominating over the decreasing forces of gravity which tend for slight expansion if acting alone, and the contraction remains amply adequate for the requirements of mountain-building. Thus this line of approach does not settle whether G is constant or not. Radar-ranging to the other terrestrial planets over a period of many years may prove decisive, but the method used involves sources of error too large for the question yet to be resolved of whether their orbits are expanding systematically and in unison. On the other hand, laser-beam ranging to the corner-reflectors placed on the Moon is of far higher accuracy, and measures to date disclose a rate of recession that closely agrees with that found from the ancient-eclipse data on the basis of a constant G.

"It is sometimes of great use in natural philosophy, to doubt of things that are commonly taken for granted; especially as the means of resolving any doubt, when once it is entertained, are often within our reach."

William Herschel

Philosophical Transactions Volume 90, 1800, p.255.

1

The Origin of the Earth

The origin of the planets of the solar system, which of course includes that of our own Earth, constitutes one of the great central problems of astronomy. Ever since the essential dynamical structure of the planetary system became revealed by the work of Kepler and above all of Newton, the problem has offered a challenge down the years which has stimulated numerous attempts at theories, and an extensive and still growing literature of the subject exists. Though most of these attempts have been unsatisfactory and inadequate, they have nevertheless been of value in leading to new lines of study, with consequent advances not only in dynamical theory but in pure mathematics requisite to the studies. Thus Laplace's equation, undoubtedly the most celebrated differential equation in mathematical physics, was first come upon in a study of the rings of Saturn, a sub-problem of the solar system of the most intransigent difficulty.

All relevant lines of evidence show inescapably that not only the Earth, but the Sun itself, cannot be infinitely old, and the phenomenon of radioactivity enables a limit to be set to the age of the Earth — at least of its outermost accessible layers — of not more than about 5,000 million years, or 5 aeons, to use the modern unit (1 aeon = 10^9 years). Of the numerous hypotheses proposed, the original nebular hypothesis of Laplace has remained, in at least some of its general features, perhaps the most enduring of all. Some of what seemed its irremediable deficiencies, however, led speculations away from it for almost a century to proposals of mechanisms of quite different style, catastrophic hypotheses as they have been termed, such as tidal encounters and actual collisions of other stars with the Sun, for example. But most of the recent theories bear a degree of resemblance in broader aspect, though not in details as will be seen, to the Laplacian scheme. In this it was supposed that the planets condensed successively as small aggregations of rings of material shed at the outermost rim of a gaseous nebula of lenticular shape, the remainder of which after formation of the whole set of planets at their appropriate distances contracted down finally into the primitive Sun. Although the process of development of the nebula was set out only descriptively, not in mathematical and physical terms, the theory at once seemed to offer the possibility of accounting for the almost coplanar character of the planetary orbits as determined by the general central plane of the nebula, and also for their nearly circular nature. At all events, the theory was accorded wide attention and considerable acceptance.

First serious misgivings arose through a study by Maxwell (of the rings of Saturn), which proved that a ring of fluid or gaseous material detached at the outer rim of a sufficiently rapidly rotating nebula would not in fact pull itself together lengthwise into a single mass, as the nebular theory supposed, but would dissipate into space. A wider question of importance, and one that can now be seen to have been impossible to deal with adequately at those times through lack of knowledge of the contents of space, was that of the origin or source of the postulated nebula itself. It would have been necessary to know that such objects actually existed somewhere at some time to render the initial postulate scientifically valid. It is to the answering of this, in a certain sense, that most modern theories have been addressed in the first place. For any hypothesis to be satisfactory, it must overcome a serious difficulty of the nebular hypothesis itself.

This is, that if any such nebula were rotating sufficiently rapidly to extend out in flattened form to the present distance of Neptune, say, the rotatory momentum of the whole mass, of which the planets now represent a little more than one-thousandth part, would have been so great that the central end-product, the primitive Sun, would have been left with far more angular momentum than the Sun possesses. Any hypothesis to be acceptable must obviously in some way avoid or overcome such a dynamical implication. In fact the Sun rotates so slowly, taking nearly as long as a month, that it shows no detectable departure from perfect sphericity.

With one of the chief claims of the nebular hypothesis shown to be invalid by so able and celebrated a theorist as Maxwell, attention seemed forced to return to catastrophic theories. Earlier than Laplace, the naturalist Buffon had already put forward the idea that some great body, quite inappropriately termed a "comet" (for astronomically these are of negligible mass), had collided with the Sun to generate the planets, but no details of any alleged mechanism were specified. Bickerton, round about 1880, seems first to have perceived, and with great enthusiasm maintained, that it would need an object itself of stellar mass to be capable of removing material from the powerful gravitational field at the solar surface, and he accordingly proposed a grazing collision of the Sun with another star as the mechanism whereby planetary material became removed. The plane of their relative motion would determine the eventual planetary plane, and the direction of this motion about the Sun producing the common directions of motion of the planets about the central body. A fatal defect attends <u>any</u> such process acting on the Sun, however, including a tidal encounter to remove material without actual material collision, for although some material might thereby be removed from the two stars, no such process could possibly endow it with more than a minute fraction of the angular momentum requisite to set it into orbital motion at planetary distances, even those of the terrestrial group, Mercury, Venus, the Earth, and Mars. Indeed, it is doubtful whether any material at all could be set into orbital motion even skimming the surface of the Sun, whereas the mighty Jupiter, carrying mass greater than all the rest of the planets put together, moves at 1000 solar-radii distance, and Neptune at about 6000 solar radii. It can be shown with a considerable degree of rigour, that material so removed must either fall back onto the surface without completing half an orbital revolution, or else escape altogether at hyperbolic speed.

It may have been some vague appreciation of these defects that moved Chamberlin & Moulton about the turn of the century to introduce their famous planetesimal theory. They supposed that even at its closest distance from the Sun the passing star moved much further out than in previous theories, yet by some sort of influence caused the Sun to eject a succession of what they termed "bolts" of material. It was claimed that ejection of these to distances of the great planets would occur on the side of the Sun nearer the passing star, and that less violent eruptions on the remoter side would project the bolts out only to the lesser distances of the terrestrial planets. The interior remnants of these bolts, which would initially be at high temperature and gaseous, were regarded as going to form initial cores of the planets-to-be, while the outer escaping parts would expand and cool and thus condense into a vast swarm of infinitesimal solid particles — termed "planetesimals" — spread out in a symmetrical disc-shaped distribution with each particle circulating in its own orbital motion round the Sun in the plane of the disc and in direction determined by the motion of the passing star, as in the Bickerton theory. Subsequent gradual gathering in of these planetesimals by the remains of the bolts, the embryo planets, would steadily circularise their initially highly eccentric orbits. The processes of the theory were presented purely verbally, but they are open to fatal objections similar to those against previous theories : there is not the slightest possibility of sufficient material being ejected, and then not in the form of "bolts", unless the star passed within a few radii of the Sun. But in that case the all-important angular momentum could not be imparted to the material, for even the passing star itself, moving with escape-speed, would have angular momentum (per unit mass) far less than that possessed by Mercury, never mind the great outer planets. However, the concept of a disc of small solid particles in individual orbital motions has proved a highly important idea, and the question is whether an acceptable mechanism can be found for forming such a disc and providing it with adequate angular momentum.

Not long after this, Jeans began to examine mathematically the possibility of purely tidal action extracting material from the Sun. His conclusion was that if a similar star passed within a few diameters, so gigantic would be the tidal wave on the solar surface (and presumably on the passing star too) that it would more or less constitute a tapering gaseous arm reaching out towards the other star. It was claimed that from the outermost tip of this arm there would become detached successive blobs of gas, mere droplets compared with the Sun itself, and it was assumed further that these primitive gaseous planets would be drawn sideways into orbital motion by the transverse gravitational pull of the receding star. A criticism was raised by Jeffreys to the effect that bodies drawn off the Sun by purely gravitational forces could not rotate more rapidly than the Sun itself, whereas the majority of the planets have angular velocities 50 or 60 times as fast. In itself, this particular objection now seems of doubtful validity, for the densities of the outer layers of the Sun, from which the planetary material was supposedly being drawn off, are far lower than those of planets, and compression down to planetary densities of the material by its self-gravitation after becoming autonomous bodies would undoubtedly speed up their rotation by a large factor. However, to overcome the supposed difficulty, a grazing collision was reverted to by Jeffreys, which would lead to a ribbon-like stream trailing out between the receding stars. In producing this, with the outer layers of the two stars necessarily sliding past one another at hundreds of kilometres per second, turbulent viscosity would generate strong vorticity in the mingling material of the filament, and when the ribbon-like stream segmented into the embryo planets through its self-gravitation, as was supposed to be the course of development, this vorticity (which is indestructible within a fluid) would lead to the necessary rapid rotations.

Before proceeding, it may be noted that much invalid criticism was levelled at both the tidal and collisional theories on the quite inadmissible grounds that the prior probability of so close an encounter of another star with the Sun was so extremely small, in view of the vastness of interstellar distances compared with the size of stars, as to rule out such a postulate. But probability is a concept only applicable to the future, and once a thing has happened, any question of its "probability" no longer arises. But this apart, with all the great number of stars in the galaxy, and its probable several billion (10^9) years greater age than the solar system, the prior probability of collision between some two stars at some time in fact borders on certainty. Our Sun, being the very one to which collision had happened is no longer a star chosen at random. In the same way, there are thousands of millions of galaxies, and again our galaxy is not one chosen at random. All that could have properly been claimed from the probability argument was that stars possessing solar systems formed by the proposed mechanism (if otherwise sound) would be extremely rare, as indeed the proponents of encounter hypotheses themselves fully realised, it may be added.

But the first person to perceive and demonstrate in dynamical terms, rather than mere words, an inescapable defect of any mechanism of collision or tidal action upon the Sun was H. N. Russell in 1935. His objection, so simple that it now seems amazing it was so long overlooked, was that on any such theory the released planetary material ought really to have angular momentum far greater than would correspond to that for an object moving in a circular orbit just outside the Sun, or even at a few solar radii from it. But a particle so moving could only be given an increase of angular momentum by increasing its speed round the Sun, and if this increase were by as little as a factor 0.42, the particle would have escape-energy and become lost from the Sun altogether, not go into a planetary orbit. The angular momentum could not be changed by a factor of $\sqrt{2}$ or more without causing it to escape. But to have any tidal effect on the Sun, the disturbing star would have to pass so close that it itself, as earlier noted, would have far less angular momentum (per unit mass) than even Mercury, which on average moves at a distance of over 80 solar radii, and therefore has nine times the angular momentum it would have if moving just above the solar surface. So even if the detached droplets (supposing such formed, which itself is doubtful) were drawn sideways to follow the departing star completely, which they obviously must not do, they would have quite inadequate angular momentum to lead to a system having the scale of the planetary orbits.

A simple means of overcoming what for a time was regarded as an insuperable difficulty was next proposed and this was to forget about the Sun as the source of planetary material and transfer the scene-of-action away from it by postulating that, prior to the existence of the planets, the Sun may have possessed a companion star similar to itself : that is, it was formerly a binary star. If a third passing star now made a suitable encounter with the companion to the Sun, material thereby removed from either or both of them would automatically have angular momentum from the outset comparable with that associated with the original orbital motion of the binary system. Examples abound in the galaxy of double-stars, a proportion with periods and separations comparable with those of the great planets and their distances from the Sun. Equally important to the theory is that the dynamical circumstances of the encounter can be such as also to bring about the complete escape of the companion-star and the passing star from the distant Sun. On such a hypothesis, all the what-seemed-then satisfactory features of the tidal or collision theories could be taken over as part of the theory, with the angular-momentum difficulty completely resolved. It is of interest to remark, in retrospect, that the time-honoured view that because the Sun is at the centre of the solar system it <u>must</u>

necessarily have been the source of the planetary material, which all theories till this last had assumed, is really little more than an illusion if not a pure mistake. For however a closed system of gravitating particles may have assembled, if one of them has a dominating mass (the Sun here) it will be little influenced by the attractions of the others and remain always close to the centre-of-mass of the system. This is an absolute dynamical necessity, and obviously not an essential indication at all of the source of the planetary material and the mode of formation.

Primitive planets, if so formed from two stars, would necessarily be at high temperature and gaseous initially, temperatures at least as high as the ordinary surface-temperatures of the encountering stars, perhaps far higher in the collisional forms of the theory, and therefore in gaseous form. But even now when in solid form, Mercury and the Moon cannot retain any substantial atmosphere, and so could never have been in gaseous form. Mars retains at present very little atmosphere, only about half a percent by mass of the terrestrial atmosphere, and if at any stage were gaseous it would have rapidly dissipated into space. Thus none of these bodies can have achieved their individuality in gaseous form, and then gone on to cool to molten form, and thence to solid form. For reasons later to be explained, it now seems settled almost beyond question that the four terrestrial planets and the Moon began their independent existence as all-solid bodies. Even for the great planets, whose present low mean-densities imply that they must be largely constituted of the lightest gases, they too must have got started by the formation within a dust-disc of all-solid cores of masses comparable with the terrestrial planets, only later becoming capable of gathering in far larger quantities of gaseous material from a surrounding nebula.

A variant of the theory dispensed with the need for any encounter by the hypothesis that the companion-star itself was initially a very close binary : numerous such triple systems have been observed to exist, thus rendering the postulate scientifically admissible.

As a result of the accretion of interstellar material by the close binary, the separation of its components would decrease, and the pair eventually coalesce into a single body which would automatically be rotationally unstable and undergo such violent asymmetrical break-up that the recoil would easily overcome the weak gravitational connection with the Sun, distant tens of astronomical units away, but leaving behind no more than a comparative wisp of material from which the planets would eventually form one-thousandth part of the combined mass of the close binary would suffice. Yet another proposal on similar lines was to the effect that the companion was only a single star but so much more massive than the Sun that it rapidly developed to the supernova-stage and material became ejected from it. Here again, the postulate is scientifically admissible, for such stellar explosions are of frequent occurrence by astronomical standards, and are responsible for generating heavy elements (needed to give terrestrial all-solid planets), and these released clouds of gas condense into vast dust-clouds that are known to abound in our galaxy and also in a great many other galaxies. Huge quantities of material, in total mass comparable with that of the Sun itself are thrown off asymmetrically in such explosions, and the recoil on the remnant star would be amply sufficient to endow it with escape-speed relative to the Sun. Material is thrown off with such violence that again only the merest wisp would or could be captured by the distant Sun.

Almost all recent theories seem to adopt the view that the first requirement is for a mechanism that would endow the Sun with a primitive nebula of dust and gas possessing adequate angular momentum about the Sun. The binary-companion and supernova-companion hypotheses would achieve this; for although in both cases the released material would be gaseous and at high temperature, expansion would cause it to cool, and those elements and compounds within it that took on the solid state at the ambient solar-maintained temperature (for instance, about 300K at the distance of the Earth) would solidify into small particles, with the remainder staying in the form of gas. If, as has recently been claimed, the nebula forms as an initial stage in the process of formation of the Sun itself, then as with the Laplace hypothesis a rapidly rotating primitive Sun would emerge. But this has been avoided by further postulating the existence of an enormously strong solar magnetic-field coupled to the planetary condensations, the rotatory momentum of the Sun thereby being transferred to the planets, driving them out to greater and greater distances. But the theory has been put forward only in verbal terms, and it is more than doubtful whether the postulates are valid and the mechanisms work in the manner claimed. Moreover, it now seems probable that the Sun is much older than the planetary system, whereas this highly speculative theory would require them to have practically the same ages.

Where non-catastrophic processes are concerned, there are several ways in which the Sun or any other star could come to acquire a gas-and-dust nebula by a more or less orderly process. Clouds of just such material exist in abundance in the galaxy, moving round in orbital motion as do the stars, and one mechanism would be by a purely dynamical effect. To simplify the matter: it is known that if three independently moving stars encounter each other with suitable initial velocities when at great distance apart, they may all eventually separate to a great distance again remaining independent, but it is also possible for two of them to become permanently bound together as a binary system while the third escapes to a great distance carrying away the excess energy. Now if one of the stars is replaced by a cloud of gas and dust, and the Sun of course one of the other two stars, then a triple encounter could result in the Sun capturing the gas-and-dust cloud by purely gravitational forces. With all the numerous stars and clouds circulating in the galaxy with slightly different velocities, there is nothing at all improbable a priori about such an event. Moreover it would only be necessary for the Sun to capture a small part of the cloud to provide enough material to form the planets. Gravitation acts just as effectively at large distances as at small distances, only with more leisurely speeds, and the passing star would not have to come unusually close to the Sun for the mechanism to work, while the clouds themselves have dimensions of the order of interstellar distances, some larger still, and masses of stellar order or greater. In any particular encounter, the precise amount of material captured and its angular momentum about the Sun, which latter is what would determine the scale of the eventual planetary system, would depend on more or less chance factors. Solar systems so formed may be extremely numerous in the galaxy, though with dimensions and planetary mass different from our own, and similarly in the very many other galaxies that contain dust-clouds.

There is an equally acceptable and even more direct way in which a star could collect dust and gas without the interaction of a second star, and this is by the process of accretion through gravitational focusing. If at one extreme the star is imagined to be at rest in such a cloud, its gravitation would draw in material radially, and if there were no net rotatory momentum associated with the cloud all its material would eventually fall to the surface of the star. But if the cloud had some such momentum, which would normally be the case, this would be conserved, and the cloud could contract only to a stage where centrifugal force (aided by pressure-gradients for the gaseous component) would counteract the attraction of the star. At the other extreme, if the star passed through the cloud at very high speed, it would collect little more than just the material it ran into bodily, and the densities and dimensions of clouds are such that the mass captured would not only be negligible but would clearly not go into orbital motion. However, somewhere between these extremes, there would be a suitable relative speed that would allow capture of mass comparable with that of the planets. This speed is of order 1 km/sec, and is small compared with relative velocities of adjacent objects in the galaxy, which for stars relative to the Sun for example are about 20 km/sec. But in the accretion-process, the star interacts gravitationally with the whole cloud, not merely with the small proportion captured, and this results in strong braking-action reducing the relative speed. Thus an initial speed of 5 km/sec could well be brought down almost to zero by this braking-action in passage of a star through a large cloud. In view of this requirement of a low relative velocity, possibly no more than 1 star in 100 has undergone an encounter suitable for capture of mass of planetary order, but this could still mean that 10^9 stars in our galaxy have planetary systems associated with them formed initially in this way. That such a process does operate in varying degree is shown by the existence of numerous comets, — there are probably several million gravitationally bound to the Sun at present, and there are groups of these that move towards the Sun from almost identical points of the celestial sphere for each group. The groups are widely spread over the whole sphere, but show a strong belt-like distribution parallel to the galactic plane and concentration about the ant-apex of the solar motion. The comets, which are vast swarms of widely-spaced dust particles, result from passages of the Sun through dust clouds at higher speeds, though still below average, and only a small amount of material compared with the mass of the planets is captured at each such encounter.

A further feature of these galactic gas-dust clouds is that they are in slow rotation sufficient to prevent them collapsing down under their self-gravitation, which means angular velocities of a few times 10^{-15} per sec. Even this seemingly minute rate implies considerable angular momentum for the captured material, and it may be shown to be of the self-same order as that carried in the orbital motions of the planets. But there is possibly a stronger source of such momentum, for not only are clouds quite irregular in form and density, but a star would be most unlikely to pass symmetrically through one. The amounts of material converging to the accretion-axis from opposite sides of some plane through it would not in general be exactly equal, and a difference as small as 1 percent would be adequate to account for the planetary angular momentum. This second source could be more effective than any original vorticity in the cloud.

Proceeding now on the assumption that the Sun has

in one of these ways acquired such a nebula with adequate angular momentum from an interstellar cloud, the nebula would necessarily contain about 1 percent by mass in the form of dust, while the remainder would be principally hydrogen. Whatever initial distribution the material may have, it will quickly develop to a special form : the dust will in fact settle into a flat disc as thin as possible with its plane perpendicular to the total-angular-momentum axis, and with each particle describing circular orbital motion round the Sun at a speed appropriate to its radial distance. To form an estimate of the thickness of this disc, if it is supposed that the whole mass of the terrestrial planets, about 1.2×10^{28} g, were distributed in a uniform circular disc extending rather beyond the orbit of Mars, say to 2.4×10^{13} cm, then if density ~ 1 g cm^3 is assumed, the thickness perpendicular to the general plane would be just under 7cm, and correspondingly less for greater density of its particles and thus of greater (volume-) density in the disc.

On the other hand, the gaseous component will extend away from this plane on both sides, for as a result of solar heating a pressure-gradient will be available to support the gas against the component of solar gravity urging it towards the equatorial plane defined by the disc of dust. Each volume-element of the gas will describe a small-circle orbit round the axis of rotational symmetry such that it maintains a constant distance to one side or other of the central plane. The half-depth of this gaseous cloud can be shown would be about 10^{12} cm at 2 AU from the Sun, and about 3×10^{13} cm at 30 AU, the present distance of Neptune. Generally, the depth increases as $R^{5/4}$ with distance R from the Sun, the reason for the increase being that the component of solar gravitation perpendicular to the plane of symmetry at a given distance from it falls off more rapidly than does the thermal energy of the gas maintained by solar heating. Dust-particles, on the other hand, are too large and dense to receive any gas-pressure support, and must therefore remain as close to the central plane as possible : if any particle were set in motion out of the plane of the dust-disc, its path would lie in a plane through the centre of the Sun, and hence would intersect the disc twice per revolution, which means that it would be absorbed into the disc by collision after completing at most half a circuit of the Sun. This is the reason why the rings of Saturn are so thin, even though containing so much less mass per unit area than the planetary disc as to be semi-transparent, and they supply inescapable observational evidence that the dust captured by the Sun would rapidly develop into as thin as possible disc-like form.

If the nebula consisted solely of gas, it would reach the same configuration as described above, broadening out from the equatorial plane with increasing distance from the Sun, but there would be no possibility whatever of planets condensing within it. With the whole mass of the planets in gaseous form filling this nebular distribution out to about the distance of Neptune, the mean density in it would be of order 10^{-13} g/cm^3. Now if a spherical condensation of density ρ, greater than this, and radius r, were to form within such a nebula at distance R from the Sun (mass M), it could only hold itself together permanently by self-gravitation against the solar disruptive tendency, if

$$\left(\frac{4}{3}\pi r^3 \rho\right)/r^2 \gg \delta(M/R^2) \doteq \frac{2Mr}{R^3}$$

where δ denotes the difference (of solar attraction) as between the centre and surface of the condensation. For R = 30 AU, this leads at once to $\rho \gg 10^{-11}$ g/cm^3, while at the distance of the Earth it requires $\rho \gg 3 \times 10^{-7}$ g/cm^3. There is no way that such local density increases could be brought about in a gas uniformly heated by solar radiation : at the distance of the Earth it would mean more than a millionfold increase. Minor irregularities, such as rarefactions and compressions, would quickly be smoothed out by the differential shearing action of the orbital motion of the gas about the general axis of rotation. But the dust-disc has entirely different properties, and aggregations can form and grow in it despite solar action precisely because its density will necessarily be that of solid material, which means a few times 1 g/cm^3, millions of times greater than the density of the gaseous component of the nebula. This feature is of the utmost importance to the process of formation of planets.

If a small body of mass m is in orbital motion round a larger one (the Sun) of mass M at distance R, it is a well-known result that its gravitational sphere of influence in competition with the Sun has radial dimension of general size $(m/3M)^{1/3}R$. For example, the Earth with mass 3×10^{-6} that of the Sun has range-of-influence about $10^{-2}R = 0.01$ AU, which is about 4 times the distance of the Moon. Were it substantially less than such a value, the lunar orbit would be unstable and the Moon sooner or later escape to become an independent planetary body. Now if a small aggregation (assumed spherical for simplicity) occurs within the dust-disc, purely by chance or by particles sticking together, and has density $\sigma \sim 1$ g/cm^3, its radius would be $(3m/4\pi\sigma)^{1/3}$. So its range-of-influence will be greater than its own physical dimensions if $R^3 > 9m/4\pi\rho$ which means $R > 10^{11}$cm about. This is less than two solar radii and smaller still if σ were greater than 1 g/cm^3; and therefore at planetary distances, which range from about 5×10^{12} to 5×10^{14} cm, the inequality will be strongly satisfied. Clearly, this results from the volume-density of the disc being that of ordinary solid material, and therefore at these distances easily capable of overcoming the solar disruptive tendency.

For particles within the range of influence of a mass m, the velocities relative to it, resulting from their orbital motions round the Sun, are small compared with those that would be needed to keep them in orbital motion about m itself, and therefore any such chance irregularity will grow by pulling in all the material of the disc within its range-of-influence. As this material is removed it will be replaced by material flowing into the (growing) sphere-of-influence from adjacent parts of the disc. It cannot be supposed that the disc will be perfectly smooth and uniform, but rather that from the outset it will possess small irregularities of thickness depending on chance details of the distribution from which it developed, and accordingly many small-scale aggregations would begin to form and increase in mass. If for simplicity it is supposed that N equal bodies have formed at a certain stage, each of mass m_p, then with the value 1.2×10^{28} g for the total mass of the disc out to about $2AU = 3 \times 10^{13}$ cm, the radius r_p of each body (making no allowance for compression) and assuming a density of about $3\ g/cm^3$ would be about $10^9 N^{1/3}$ cm. Each of these bodies would of course be in orbit round the Sun, and while N remained large there would obviously be much congestion resulting in collisions. Even without mutual perturbations, a separate circular orbit for each one would not begin to be possible until the sum of their N diameters became less than 3×10^{13} cm, and this would require $N \leqslant 1.8 \times 10^6$. The corresponding radius would be given by $r_p = 8 \times 10^6$ cm and the mass $m_p = 7 \times 10^{21}$ g, a sizeable mass, but still small by planetary standards (about one-millionth that of the Earth, for example). In fact, strictly circular orbits would not be possible because of gravitational interactions, and collisions would certainly occur that would further disturb the orbits from circular form. Loss of energy in bodily collisions would lead to build-up of larger masses still by the coalescence of the two bodies involved, and any debris ejected in such collisions would simply add to what was left unaccumulated of the original disc, to be later gathered in by the larger masses.

It is a general principle that any dynamical system possessing a means of dissipating energy within itself will evolve to its state of lowest possible energy. But an autonomous system cannot get rid of its angular momentum by any internal mechanism. In the present instance, the first stage is for the dust to move quite rapidly to the disc-like distribution, which clearly is achieved by loss of gravitational energy (as formation of the disc involves collisions). The time for this to occur is of the same order as the orbital period about the Sun at the distance concerned, and thus about a year for the material eventually destined to form the terrestrial planets. The next stage is the further much greater dissipation of energy that can be achieved by the disc aggregating into compact bodies and this will proceed until there are few enough of them for collisions practically to cease. There will eventually result just a few large bodies that have successfully swept their local annular zones almost completely clear and are no longer sufficiently perturbed by their neighbouring rival large masses to undergo further collisions particularly with them. The process is an exponentially decaying one, never quite concluded, but with a comparatively short half-life of only about 10^4 years. It still continues at an infinitesimal rate, and there remain small asteroids with orbits passing close to that of the Earth which will eventually be swept up and absorbed into the planet. Very small bodies, in the shape of meteorites, are continually falling to Earth from interplanetary orbits, but now adding negligibly to its mass. It can be shown that the time taken for the Earth to have grown by this mechanism to 90% of its present mass would have been about 2.4×10^4 years, to 99% about 4.2×10^4 years, and to 99.9% in about 4.7×10^4 years, and so on.

As the material of the disc became more and more depleted, small embryo planets would obviously cease to have any source for serious further growth, and unless captured in collision by one of the larger bodies would remain as dwarf-planets. It is entirely possible that at some early stage the Moon had grown practically to its present mass as an independent planet in an orbit close to that of the still-growing Earth while at least a small proportion of the disc-material remained unabsorbed. If then the Moon were temporarily captured by the Earth, which can happen purely dynamically under the combined gravitational influence of the Sun, the slightest addition of mass to <u>either</u> body, which would still have been occurring, would reduce their mutual distance and lock them together permanently bound by gravitation. The large craterings, the so-called <u>seas</u>, on the Moon are the visible remains of the impacts of the smaller but still comparatively large bodies that finally went to make up its mass. The initial distance of the Moon captured in this way would have been more than three times its present value, but further growth of the bodies would reduce this distance : increase of mass of the Moon by one-quarter, for example, would halve the distance even if the Earth were not continuing to grow.

Two other highly important consequences follow from this mode of formation of the planets. First, their rotations are readily explicable by the fact that in virtue of the general Keplerian motion round the Sun of every element of the disc, its material must possess vorticity just as if it were a fluid. It is a well-known theorem in hydrodynamics that if a small spherical volume-element of a fluid were suddenly to be solidified without change of density, it would immediately thereafter rotate with angular velocity equal to the local value of the vorticity. If the shape is not spherical, the relationship is less simple because of unequal moment-of-inertia factors, but the subsequent angular velocity is of much the same magnitude and sign as the vorticity. In the present case, the vorticity vector for any element of the disc is in the same sense as the orbital angular velocity or angular momentum, and this means that condensations, if formed perfectly symmetrically, would rotate in precisely the same sense as the rotatory motion of the disc. It can be shown that the process of growth would be capable of producing initial rotation periods of the order of a few hours, depending on the range from which condensations were able to gather in material, the more massive the planet the greater the range would become, as has been seen, and the shorter the rotation-period.

Both Mercury and Venus now rotate exceptionally slowly. Without going into the problems thereby raised in any depth here, this could be accounted for to a large extent by tidal action of the Sun over billions of years, though it remains quite uncertain exactly what initial angular velocities were possessed by most if not all of the planets. For example, where the Earth is concerned, ancient-eclipse data supply almost inescapable evidence that the day is now lengthening as a result of tidal action of the Moon and Sun, the rotatory momentum lost from the Earth reappearing as orbital angular momentum in the Earth-Moon system. But the present rate of recession of the Moon is such that if extrapolated back in time, the distance would have been comparable with the radius of the Earth only about 1.5 aeons ago, a quite unacceptable result, with the Earth carrying the bulk of the angular momentum by rotating in about 5 hours. The difficulty suggests either that tidal action may not have been anything like as strong in long-past times, or that some other effect acts to reduce the lunar distance, one not operating at the present time, and vitiating a conclusion based on tidal theory only, but it would be digressing too far to consider the possibilities here. That Mars rotates in a period closely similar to that of the Earth yet has no massive satellite may not constitute any problem, for it has mass only one-ninth that of the Earth, and thus because of its smaller range-of-action and the smaller vorticity in the disc at its distance from the Sun would be likely to have smaller initial angular velocity than the Earth. Also there are no seas or oceans on Mars to produce friction from solar tides to slow the rotation, and the present rotation of Mars may well not be very different from its initial rate.

The seemingly strangest anomaly in the solar system is presented by Uranus with a rotation-axis inclined at about 98° to the direction of the pole of its orbit. The period is just under 11 hours, not much longer than those of Saturn and Jupiter. The curious direction is clearly inconsistent with gradual growth of a single body in the original solar nebula, and a reasonable explanation would be that at some fairly late stage in the accretion of the nebula, two separate planets of comparable mass came into collision and coalesced to form a single body. In such an event, the final rotation-vector would be determined by the sum not only of the former angular-momentum vectors of the two planets but also that associated with their relative hyperbolic motion just before collision. This motion could even be retrograde, and the final outcome could be an angular-momentum vector in almost any direction, quite minor circumstances determining the precise orientation of the axis of the final single body.

The second important consequence of the fact that the thickness of the dust-disc will at all stages have been infinitesimally small compared with the diameter of any incipient planet is that captured material would necessarily fall to its surface only in a narrow great-circle band, and not at all parts of the surface as has usually been assumed in discussions of the growth of planets by accretion. On impact, the translational energy of infall is randomised to reappear as heating of the materials directly involved in the collision, and that this occurs only in a narrow band a few centimetres wide defined by the dust-disc makes a crucial difference from the case where it is supposed to rain down all over the surface simultaneously.

To obtain an estimate of the energies and temperatures that would be involved : the kinetic energy of unit-mass of material falling from great distance to the surface of a spherical mass m of radius r_m is Gmr_m^{-1} (where G is the constant of gravitation). Hence unit-mass falling in will add energy at the surface, at an upper-limit rate E given by

$$E(\text{per gram arriving}) = G(4\pi\rho/3)^{1/3}\, m^{2/3}\,,$$

where ρ is the density of the planet, which for order-of-magnitude purposes may be assumed to remain constant as m increases. For a body approaching the present mass of the Moon, a suitable value of m would be 6×10^{25} g, and if $\pi\rho = 10$ g/cm^3 is adopted as the density, then the numerical value of E is 2.4×10^{10} erg/g. Now the energy required to liquefy rocky material consists of a latent-heat-of-fusion of about 100 cal/g together with the energy needed to raise the temperature by about 1200°C. For a specific heat of 0.2 cal per °C per gram, this would mean a total of 340 cal/g, or 1.4×10^{10} erg/g. Thus infalling material would possess kinetic energy sufficient to liquefy it if rather more than half the above maximum figure were converted into heat in the material. It would of course be stopped in its motion by surface-material and share its energy with that involved. Thus when a planet had grown to about the size of the Moon, the energy of infall would be just about sufficient to bring about liquefaction of the materials directly concerned.

But the energy so brought in would be delivered only to an extremely narrow great-circle band, as already emphasised, and the liquefied material would clearly flow sideways from the band in polarward directions. It could not simply pile up indefinitely along the band, either as liquid or solid, for gravitation would sooner or later bring the surface as near to an equipotential form as possible. The melted material by spreading itself out in this way would also produce a distribution especially conducive to its cooling, not only because of its thinness and areal extent enabling it to radiate away its thermal energy, but because once moved away from the great-circle band of infall it would receive no infalling material to maintain or add to its heat. It would take at most only a matter of minutes for material spread out in this way to cool sufficiently by radiation to re-solidify. The important conclusion emerges that planets formed in this thin disc would necessarily build up to this stage as bodies solid throughout. Discussion of the evolution of these primitive bodies to planets, the Earth in particular, must therefore be constrained to the assumption of an all-solid initial state.

Some change in details of the process would come about as the mass continued to increase, for the infall energy increases as $m^{2/3}$, and therefore the heating would reach sufficient intensity to volatilise at least some of the incoming materials that the dust-disc might contain. When this occurred, the effect would gradually be to envelope the growing planet in a shielding atmosphere, through which subsequently arriving dust particles would fall more or less as meteors do, though still necessarily in a narrow great-circle band. In passage through this atmosphere, they would undergo heating and ablation, and the process would enable their energy of infall to be disposed of with little or no addition of heat at the solid surface, for some of the energy would be radiated away as light, just as for ordinary meteors in the present terrestrial atmosphere, while the minute micro-meteors resulting from ablation would descend through the atmosphere at low terminal speeds transferring their energy to it by viscous drag and bringing negligible energy to the surface. When it had grown sufficiently, such an atmosphere would entirely shield the solid surface from receiving any of the infall-energy of small particles, but it would not prevent the continued increase of the mass of the body as the result of the more refractory substances reaching the surface as micro-meteors in solid form.

Larger bodies accumulated in the disc, if sufficiently massive, would be able to penetrate this atmosphere almost with free-fall speed. But it is quite certain that energy so delivered must be accommodated at once in the neighbourhood of the impact. When a meteorite strikes the lunar surface, its energy is not communicated to the whole body of the Moon to heat it up throughout but forms a localised impact-crater. Some melting occurs if the relative speed is high enough at and near the interface between meteorite and lunar surface-material, but this rapidly cools and resolidifies by radiating away the energy into space. But, as aforesaid, this activity takes place in the immediate neighbourhood of the impact area, as is evidenced by the lunar craters, and does not lead to the general heating of the growing body. Thus at every stage of the mechanism of formation of a planet, initially from particles of the dust-disc, later from infall of moderate-sized accumulations within the disc, and onwards to the infall of bodies of asteroidal dimensions, there would be no important heating of the planet.

This conclusion is of course the complete opposite of the view that dominated cosmogonical belief for generations, according to which the terrestrial planets formed in some way as first to be gaseous and then later molten throughout. But, as has already been seen, there can really be no possibility of the Moon and Mercury, and probably Mars, ever having been other than solid everywhere within them, while considerations that will duly be arrived at later connected with the existence of mountains on Earth entirely substantiate the conclusion that all the terrestrial planets and the Moon began their independent existences as bodies sufficiently cool to be solid throughout.

The four great outer planets, Jupiter, Saturn, Uranus, and Neptune, will not be the concern of the subsequent chapters of this volume, nor their numerous satellites and the curious small object Pluto. However, it may be briefly noticed that since gravitational condensation from the gaseous nebula itself is not directly possible even at the distance of Neptune, it must follow that these giant-planets — Jupiter at 317 Earth-masses down to Uranus at 15 Earth-masses — could have commenced to form only within a dust-disc extending out to their distances. Thus the present central parts of these objects can be expected to consist of small cores of much the same compositions as the terrestrial planets, and if the present total of their masses corresponds more or less to the whole mass of the original nebula, then it is probable that about one percent of their masses, the proportion of dust in the nebula, would have gone to form the initially solid cores, though as will be seen later by analogy with the Earth this central material is likely now to be in liquid rather than solid form owing to the high central pressures in the great planets. In the case of Jupiter, this would mean a core of about 3 Earth-masses, for Saturn about 1 Earth-mass, while for both Uranus and Neptune about the present mass of Mars, which seem reasonably satisfactory estimates.

Such cores having developed, there then becomes no difficulty in regard to their capturing and retaining the gaseous components of the nebula despite its low volume-density. At the present distance of the Earth from the Sun, the temperature is such that a hydrogen-atmosphere could with difficulty be held by the planet for any length of time, but if the Earth were placed ten times as far away, roughly at the distance of Saturn, it could hold such an atmosphere easily, for escape of gas depends on the thermal energy of its particles as supplied by the Sun. A planet of mass three times the Earth could readily retain a hydrogen atmosphere at the distance of Jupiter. Thus once solid cores of sufficient mass had been formed, there would be no difficulty in their gradually collecting in the gaseous component contributing much the greater part by mass and volume of the solar nebula. In doing so, the intrinsic vorticity of the gaseous nebular material would account for the rotations of the planets as before, the lessening amount of vorticity, which falls off as $R^{-3/2}$ with distance R from the Sun, being offset by greater range-of-influence of such massive planets.

REFERENCES AND NOTES

This chapter is intended only as a brief outline of the history of the problem from Laplace to the present. The main conclusion emerging is that the terrestrial planets, the Earth in particular, achieved their individual existences as bodies in practically all-solid form, thus imposing this initial boundary-condition on their courses of evolution. That these planets cannot have evolved from all-gaseous to molten and solid form receives direct support from the absence of any substantial atmospheres on the Moon and Mercury. The escape of an atmosphere is an exponential process which occurs very rapidly or extremely slowly according to the relation of thermal velocities to escape-velocities. (The tenuous atmosphere associated with Mercury probably represents only a condensational balance within the surrounding interplanetary gases.)

Alfven H. & Arrhenius G. Evolution of the Solar System, NASA, Washington DC, 1976.
This contains an extensive list of references pp.505-529; and further references for each year may be found in the following annual publication:

Astronomy & Astrophysics Abstracts, Springer-Verlag, Berlin.

Fowler R.H. Statistical Mechanics, Cambridge, 1929.
Contains improved theory by E.A.Milne and others of escape of atmospheres.

Jeans J.H. Dynamical Theory of Gases, Cambridge, 1916.
This contains an early attempt on the problem of escape of atmospheres.

Jeans J.H. Problems of Cosmogony and Stellar Dynamics, Cambridge, 1919.

Jeans J.H. Astronomy and Cosmogony, Cambridge, 1929.

Lyttleton R.A. Dynamical Calculations Relating to the Origin of the Solar System, Mon.Not.Roy.Astron.Soc. 121, 551, 1960.

Lyttleton R.A. Effect on the Lunar Orbit of Meteoritic Accretion, Icarus 1, 137, 1962 & 5, 162, 1966.

Lyttleton R.A. Dynamical Capture of the Moon by the Earth, Proc.Roy.Soc. A 296, 243, 1967.

Lyttleton R.A. On the Formation of Planets from a Solar Nebula, Mon.Not.Roy.Astron.Soc., 158, 463, 1972.

Russell H.N. The Solar System and Its Origin, Macmillan 1935.

Schmidt, Otto. A Theory of Earth-Origin, Moscow, 1958.

Tyror J.G. Distribution of Perihelia of Long-Period Comets, Mon.Not.Roy.Astron.Soc. 117, 370, 1957.
The distribution is shown to have vanishingly small prior probability of randomness, and close association with the solar apex and with the galactic plane was established. More recently the remarkable concentration of perihelia near the solar apex has been inescapably demonstrated by Hasaegawa I., (Publ. Astron Soc. Japan 28, 259, 1976). Again, assuming a girdle-distribution of perihelia, even closer association with the galactic plane (than found by Tyror) has been demonstrated by Mardia K.V. (Journ. Roy. Stat. Soc. 37, 363, 1975).

2

The Interior of the Earth

Where the internal constitution of the Earth is concerned, radioactivity is of extremely high importance. As is now well known, radioactivity arises from spontaneous changes in the nuclear structure of certain atoms, whereby α-particles (helium nuclei), β-particles (electrons), and γ-rays will be emitted, always with very high energies. The interactions of these emissions with any surrounding material result in a general absorption of their energy which contributes to the heat of that material. For the Earth, the process manifests itself immediately in the form of an increase of temperature with depth. The temperature at the surface is maintained almost wholly by solar radiation, but beyond moderate distance below the surface where variations of temperature no longer occur, there is at first a rapid increase with depth. The average temperature-gradient, determined from numerous borings and in mines, is as high as 20°C per kilometre, but individual gradients range from about 30°C per km at places in Europe down to only about 10°C per km in South African mines, which small rate compared with most gradients elsewhere enables mining to be conducted there at correspondingly greater depths. On the other hand, the associated outflow of heat to the surface shows rather smaller variation from place to place, the conductivity tending to be roughly in inverse proportion to the temperature-gradient. The average heat-flow is somewhere near 50 erg/cm^2 sec, but values at different parts of the globe range mainly over about 40–80 erg/cm^2 sec. The outflow of heat just below the ocean floor, from such measures as have yet been made, appears not to be significantly smaller than at land-stations. Less than a century ago, it was confidently believed that the solid outer crust was at most 50 km thick with the entire interior remaining 99% in molten form, but this was before studies of seismic waves were to show the absurdly erroneous nature of this naive picture.

It is certain that the source of this heat is radioactivity, for the associated rocks can be analysed chemically and their content of radioactive elements determined. The relevant principal constituents are one of the isotopes of uranium ^{238}U, thorium ^{232}Th, and an isotope of potassium ^{40}K. Although numerous elements are radioactive in some degree, only the foregoing are of importance geophysically because their decay-times are comparable with the age of the Earth and they thus still remain active. The decay-time τ of a radioactive element may be defined to be such that if at time $t = 0$ there is a mass q_o of the element, then at later time t the remaining mass will be $q = q_o \exp(-t/\tau)$. The following Table shows these times τ and the energy emitted per gram of the element per year as a result of the decay.

TABLE 1

Element	Decay-time τ	Heat produced (erg/g/year)
^{238}uranium U	6.75×10^9 yrs	3.06×10^7
^{232}thorium Th	1.89×10^{10} yrs	0.84×10^7
^{40}potassium K	1.82×10^9 yrs	1.09×10^3

The heat-production near the surface depends on the type of rock locally present, granites and basalts contributing most, and of course depends on the amounts of these radioactive elements contained in them. Uranium and thorium are extremely rare elements, and typical rocks contain only of order a few parts per million by mass, but K is much less rare and so makes a moderate contribution to the heating despite its much weaker rate of energy-emission. The following values for the radioactive generation of heat in ergs per gram per year for the most typical rocks are given by Allen (1973) to be as follows :

TABLE 2

	U	Th	K	Total (erg/g/yr)
Granitic	109	92	29	230
Basaltic	25	29	8	63

Taking into account minute quantities of these elements in other types of rocks, the total release is about 295 erg / g/yr, but the figures represent only rough average values, and the actual releases differ from place to place both with depth and horizontal distance.

Now it is plain that if a temperature-gradient of 20°C per km continued down indefinitely, there would soon be reached enormously high temperatures by ordinary everyday standards. The radius of the Earth is over 6,371 km, and extrapolation would imply central temperature in excess of 100,000°C. Even at the base of the solid mantle, a depth of 2,898 km, it would mean almost 60,000°C, probably hot enough to melt any substance even at the high pressure prevailing there (of 1.37 x 10^{12} dyn/cm^2). Calculation of the rate of increase of the melting-point with depth, owing to the increasing pressure, shows it to be only about 1°C per km (Shimazu Y. : 1954). Since the surface-value of the melting-point for most rocks is about 1300°C, this would imply a value as low as only about 4300°C near the base of the solid mantle. Even with the rather higher estimate of 3°C per km obtained many years ago by Jeffreys (who, however, now considers the smaller value to be more nearly correct), the melting-point would still reach only 10,000°C at the base of the mantle. The conclusion is inescapable on any basis that the radioactive content by mass in the outer layers cannot continue on down beyond about 20 km depth.

Recent in-situ measures of thermal gradients at a few points of the lunar surface, made possible by the Apollo-missions, show them to be unexpectedly high (Proc. Lunar Sci. Conf. 1976, 1977), and begin to suggest that the outer layers may resemble those of the Earth in having far higher radioactive content than the interior below a few kilometres depth. There is no possibility of the Moon having such radioactive content throughout as would yield 250 erg/g year or anywhere near that on average. The pressure at the centre of the Moon is only 0.048×10^{12} dyn/cm^2 and the melting point there could be as high as 1900°C (Chap.5, p.104). Since typical rocks have latent-heat of fusion of about 100 cal/g and specific-heat of about 0.2 cal/g per °C, about 2×10^{10} erg per gram would be required to melt material at the centre of the Moon, and progressively less at smaller depths. If 250 erg/g year were being released, this amount would be supplied in less than 10^8 years, and subsequently being added to, even at gradually decreasing rate, would maintain the Moon in liquid form throughout almost indefinitely, despite some escape of the energy at the surface through conduction upwards. Similarly for Mars, the central pressure is small and less than 0.3×10^{12} dyn/cm^2, and with this rate of energy-release melting would reach the centre in less than 3×10^8 years, and thereafter such rate would maintain the whole planet (surface-layers apart, perhaps) in liquid form, escape of energy at the surface, per unit mass of the planet, being considerably less than for the Moon. But there is every reason to suppose that the Moon and Mars are solid throughout, which implies that no more than an average of 10-20 erg/g year can have been released in their interiors by long-life radioactive elements at any stage.

The density-distribution of currently radioactive materials in the extreme outer layers of the Earth must be far greater than throughout the remainder : indeed, as already noted, a thickness of 20 km depth would release enough energy to account for the whole outflow of heat coming to the surface. Such a layer would contain only about 0.5 per cent of the whole mass of the Earth. Now in the general distribution of the elements (formed probably in supernova-explosions), all elements occur to some extent but in different proportions, and it would be impossible here to assume that the remaining 99.5 per cent of the terrestrial mass is completely devoid of these radioactive elements with half-lives in excess of 10^9 years. It has been estimated by MacDonald (1959) that they would have been present originally to such amount as to release energy at the rate of about 20 erg/g year. If an average value to the present time is adopted of 10 erg/g year, then in 4.5×10^9 years (the currently accepted age of the Earth) this could raise the temperature by something approaching 5000°C, which as has been seen is roughly the melting-point temperature at the base of the mantle. Nevertheless, this value of 10 erg/g year would mean that unit mass of material in the deep interior contained only a few per cent of the amount of these radioactive elements contained in unit mass of the outer layers, and the problem arises of how such a remarkable difference and non-uniform distribution can have come about.

On the ancient hypothesis that the Earth first achieved its individuality in gaseous form followed by a molten stage, the problem was considered to be readily soluble by the suggestion that uranium and thorium atoms are of such dimensions that they would not fit into the lattices of any silicate crystals, and would therefore remain dissolved in lighter materials which would rise to the surface as a result of hydrostatic differentiation. But with the Earth starting in all-solid form, such an explanation obviously becomes inadmissible. As mentioned above, the few measures of heat-flow and radial temperature-gradients at the lunar surface indicate that the outer layers have similarly high radioactive content. A distinct possibility is that these layers may have been added some time after the initial formation of the Earth and Moon as individual slightly smaller bodies, as a result of a further encounter with a quite separate interstellar dust-cloud possessing the necessary high content of these radioactive elements. It is possible that such mass, added at a later stage with different angular-momentum vector about the Sun, would contribute at least in part to the orbital inclinations of the planets.

Analyses of rocks to determine the content of the various product-elements of radioactive breakdown within them are regarded as affording the most reliable means of finding the so-called age of the Earth. But rocks used for this are of necessity selected from present surface or near-surface materials : rocks known for certain to be from depths greater than 20 km are not available : and this means that ages determined by reliance on radioactive processes may relate only to a comparatively shallow layer added to an already existing older Earth. Were the Sun, together with a retinue of aready-formed planets, to pass through an interstellar dust-cloud in such circumstances as to acquire another but lesser dust-disc, with angular momentum sufficient to maintain it at planetary distances, ther is no doubt that this would soon be swept up by the existing planetary masses. Interstellar dust is considered to be the product of supernova-explosions that follow from processes within stars in which heavy elements are generated from lighter ones. Once released into space and allowed to cool, all radioactive elements so formed would proceed to decay at their individual rates, those of short half-lives developing quickly to stable atoms, those of longer lifetimes remaining in higher proportions, and so on to those with lifetimes measured in aeons. Some interstellar clouds may be of comparatively recent origin and thus their content of U, Th, and K not decayed substantially, while others may have existed as clouds in the galaxy for billions of years since first scattered into space, and thus have low content of U, Th, and K. Also, the proportions of the various elements initially formed in a supernova would depend on detailed factors prior to the explosion, as for example the mass and angular momentum of the original body, which would be different from one star to another, and this again could influence the final abundance-ratios. Discouraging as it may be to have to recognise this, it seems entirely possible that the ages so far found by the medium of radioactivity may relate only to the outer layers representing perhaps less than one per cent of the whole Earth by mass, and if this is so "the age of the Earth" becomes a less definite concept.

Before proceeding, it may be worth mentioning that some light could well be thrown on the question if samples of cometary material could be recovered and age-dated, or, less likely, their ages determined in situ by means of rendezvous-missions. There is strong evidence that comets represent aggregations of interstellar dust formed by the process of solar gravitational focussing when the Sun passes through a gas-and-dust cloud at moderate speed. Such clouds are extremely numerous in the galaxy, and in their overall extent occupy something like 15 per cent of its volume, though they are concentrated towards the galactic plane. Every few million years or so, but at random intervals, passage of the solar system must occur through a different cloud to produce a fresh accession of comets. Unfortunately in the present connection, if they do not fall directly into the Sun, such comets necessarily begin as so-called long-period comets, and their subsequent arrivals in the inner parts of the solar system, where only then would they be accessible from Earth with present energy-capabilities, are quite unpredictable as yet, and often such comets appear and disappear again in a matter of months. Accordingly, spacecraft-missions to these objects remain highly improbable undertakings in the foreseeable future, requiring as they would a spacecraft to be more or less always at the ready in the hope of a suitable long-period comet presenting itself.

Actual determination of the age of the Earth is a problem with a long and chequered history. It is no longer necessary to aim at quite such precision as that of the claim that "the world was created on 22 October 4004 B.C. at 6 o'clock in the evening", - indeed even an accuracy within ten-million years is far from present attainment - though this is not to deny that some omniscient power might have created it at that date and hour (G.M.T.?) with all the properties needed to deceive innocent scientists into thinking that the Earth is billions of years old and the universe itself perhaps infinitely old. Clearly what is needed for the purpose is some steadily occurring process, analogous to a clock winding down from a known initial state, to measure some unidirectional secular effect, and several methods have been suggested of widely differing degrees of reliability. For instance, the increase of salinity of the seas from rivers and deposition from the atmosphere, the laying down of sedimentary rocks, and the cooling of the Earth (from an assumed initial all-molten state) have been discussed down the ages without achieving any serious success. Dynamical considerations of possible secular changes in the planetary orbits at one time seemed hopeful, but the method is now known to be doomed to failure, and the evolution of the lunar orbit has been given great attention. But as will be seen later, although the present rate associated with this last process can be reasonably accurately determined, other vitiating factors must have entered at times, and the method fails to set any definite age to the Earth, or even the Earth-Moon system. Knowledge of the evolution and age of the Sun itself could obviously do no more than supply an upper limit for the Earth, and in the same way the rate of expansion of the universe has been regarded as leading to an upper limit, but the present values of these limits are so great as to place no serious restriction on the age of the Earth.

By far the most reliable method of age-determinations is by means of the radioactive content of suitable rocks, for radioactivity is a process the rate of which can be measured with high accuracy, and is unaffected by ordinary influences such as pressure and temperature or by chemical combination of the atoms concerned. Here again, uranium-238, ^{238}U, with its long decay-time, is of special importance, as also is uranium-235, ^{235}U, with a shorter decay-time of 1.02×10^9 years. An atom of ^{238}U breaks down through a series of stages, emitting in all 8 α-particles (helium nuclei) before becoming an atom of lead-206, ^{206}Pb. The rate of decay is such that given 1 gram of pure ^{238}U, then after 10^9 years there will remain only

0.862 g of the ^{238}U, the part 0.138 g of the mass having transmuted into ^{4}He and ^{206}Pb. After 4.5×10^9 yrs, which is a current estimate for the age of the Earth, the mass of ^{238}U remaining would be 0.513 g. Similarly for 1 gram of thorium-232, ^{232}Th, the corresponding values are 0.949 grams for the thorium remaining after 10^9 yrs, and 0.788 grams after 4.5×10^9 years. These figures illustrate, in passing, that the rate of radioactive heat production in the interior of the Earth would still be more than half the initial rate, and thus of continuing importance.

The initial and final elements in these radioactive processes may be set out thus :

$$^{238}U \rightarrow {}^{206}Pb + 8\ He,$$

$$^{235}U \rightarrow {}^{207}Pb + 7\ He,$$

$$^{232}U \rightarrow {}^{208}Pb + 6\ He.$$

It is seen therefore that in principle chemical analysis of a piece of rock that determines the proportion by mass of ^{238}U to that of ^{206}Pb, would lead to a value for the time-interval since the material contained no ^{206}Pb. In practice, difficulties enter in that the rock specimen may contain some original lead, and a chemical analysis not distinguishing between different isotopes would yield an overestimate of the age. On the other hand, an analysis for the helium-content may give too low an age if any of the gas has escaped by diffusion through the rock. But with careful selection of rocks not prone to such hindering effects, the difficulties can be overcome.

The ages of many eruptive rocks have been measured by such means, and are found to accord with the epochs that had already been settled geologically from the strata in which the rocks were resident. For example, the ages determined for Carboniferous rocks are 2.5×10^8 years; and for the oldest pre-Cambrian about 1.5×10^9 years. With continued application of various methods depending on radioactivity, and with considerable improvement in techniques, the greatest ages established have steadily increased, and some of the oldest specimens analysed to date are found to have ages of about 4×10^9 years. These ages all along the line have been confirmedby means of a number of variants of thegeneral radioactive method. A definite upper limit would seem to emerge from the fact that for different isotopes of the same element, those atoms of even atomic-weight are more numerous than those of an odd atomic-weight, and thus ^{238}U-atoms should always have been more plentiful than ^{235}U-atoms. The present ratio can be found by analysis and according to Holmes (1965) is just about 140:1. Using the values given above for their decay-times, the two isotopes would have been equally numerous a little less than 6×10^9 years ago. This figure would therefore appear to be an extreme upper limit to the age of the surface-layers. If in fact their age is 4.5×10^9 years, then the initial ratio of number of atoms of ^{238}U to ^{235}U would have been about 3.3:1. The combined outcome of the various determinations based upon radioactivity-methods would seem to be converging to a value not greatly different from 4.5×10^9 years, though there can be no certainty that further determinations may not increase the age possibly as high as 5×10^9 years.

Attention is next turned to what has been revealed about the interior of the Earth from the study of earthquake waves. It is well known that the velocities of the primary and secondary waves in a homogeneous solid, the so-called P-waves and S-waves, are related to the rigidity μ, the bulk-modulus k, and the density ρ, as follows:

$$v_P^2 = \frac{\frac{4}{3}\mu + k}{\rho}, \qquad v_S^2 = \frac{\mu}{\rho}, \qquad \dots. (1)$$

and hence that the bulk-modulus, or <u>incompressibility</u>, of the material is related to the wave-velocities by

$$\frac{k}{\rho} = v_P^2 - \frac{4}{3} v_S^2 . \qquad \dots. (2)$$

From the seismic data the values of the primary and secondary velocities of earthquake-waves, v_P and v_S, have been determined at all depths within the Earth consistently with certain model-distributions of the mass. The models arrived at differ in some of their details, but the main features are very much the same for all (Bullen 1965). In order to account for recorded travel-times with highest attainable accuracy, Bullen with some elaboration has divided the Earth into seven consecutive zones denoted in order of depth by A, B, C, D, E, F, and G. But some of these are so small in range of depth and volume that for present purposes they can be included as part of adjacent far larger zones. For example, region-A refers to the outermost crustal layers from the free surface down to depth about 33 km, and together with region-B forms what is termed the outer-shell, which extends to a depth of 413 km. Here there occurs a phase-change to a denser crystal form, the level being referred to as the 20°-discontinuity, at which the pressure is 0.141×10^{12} dyn per cm^2. The next region C is of the nature of a small transition-zone ranging from 413 km depth to 984 km, and merges into region-D which constitutes the main body of the solid mantle extending to depth 2898 km. Region-C occupies less than 4 per cent of the combined volumes of C and D, less still of their combined mass, and by adopting averaged values for the elastic properties, these regions can be taken together as comprising the solid mantle, the pressure at the base of which is 1.37×10^{12}dyn per cm^2. Here there occurs across the mantle-core boundary a sharp transition from solid-form in the mantle to metallic liquid-form in the core, and this is accompanied by a discontinuous increase of density from 5.68 g/cm^3 in the mantle to 9.43 g/cm^3 in the core, that is by a factor of 1.66, which as will be seen later is significant in exceeding a critical value of 1.5.

The core has a total mass of 1.876×10^{27}g, which is 31.4 per cent of that of the whole Earth, and there is evidence that it consists of three zones labelled E, F, and G by Bullen. The outer region E, which is certainly liquid, lies between radial distances 3473 km and 1389 km from the centre; next comes a shallow transition-layer F from 1389 km to 1250 km; and finally the innermost core G of radius 1250 km. These three zones occupy respectively 93.6, 1.75, and 4.66 per cent of the whole volume of the core, and here again it is possible to allow for the small regions F and G by slight averaging to be included with E as constituting the core. In terms of the volume of the whole Earth, the regions E, F, and G occupy respectively 15.16, 0.28, and 0.76 per cent, which makes even clearer the very small contribution of F and G, and the validity of including them with E by suitable averaging of their properties for the purposes of general discussion of the evolution of the Earth.

By such means, the planet can be represented with only slight simplification as consisting of three main zones : first, a liquid core ; second, a surrounding all-solid mantle ; and third, a solid outer-shell. The uses that will be made in the sequel of this model will be limited to general broad properties, such as the values of the radius, the changes in moment-of-inertia, and in the gravitational energy at different stages of evolution. The values for the relevant physical properties of the interior of the Earth for such purposes can be determined by least-squares representation of the known values of k, p, and ρ in the three zones, and it can be verified reversely that a model-Earth so defined would have almost exactly the actual radius and moment-of-inertia of the Earth, together with the dimensions and masses of the three zones, and also the pressures at the interfaces between them. There is little or no leeway in the appropriate quantities, and there is negligible change in the results that depend on them, which will be given in Ch.6, if any similarly defined model is adopted. Indeed, it will be shown later that even if the mantle and outer-shell are taken together as a single zone, with their combined mass having the properties of mantle-material, the changes of overall-radius, of moment-of-inertia, and of gravitational energy along a series of such 2-zone models are not importantly different from the changes along a corresponding series of 3-zone models.

Where the details of the elastic properties are concerned, first may be mentioned an interesting property of the bulk-modulus k, which is made clear when its values are plotted against the pressure, not against depth as is usually done. It is then obvious that a linear empirical relation exists, and thus that the known seismic data for k and p satisfy with extremely high accuracy a relation of the form

$$k = a + bp \qquad ....(3)$$

where a and b are certain constants, but having <u>different</u> values in each zone. It turns out that b, which is a pure number, is close to 3.5 in both the mantle and core, and not greatly different from this in the outer-shell, a result that probably has some theoretical significance where the properties of matter at high pressures of order 10^{12} dyn/cm^2 are concerned, as will be seen in a later chapter discussing the Ramsey phase-change hypothesis.

In Table 3 are shown the velocities of the P and S waves, and the values of k, p, and ρ taken from the Jeffreys-Bullen seismic data, at a series of depths in the Earth mainly at intervals of 100 km and 200 km, as seen. The plot of k against p obtained from these values is shown in Fig. 1, and the two straight lines are of $k = a + 3.5p$ for the mantle and core. A linear law is so closely satisfied in each zone that in presenting the (k,p)-diagram the straight lines had to be drawn in segments in order that the great majority of the points would not be concealed by the lines themselves, if drawn continuous, so extremely close is the linear fit, as may be seen from inspection of Fig. 1. It turns out to be convenient to use the form (3) for k, but where numerical calculations are concerned it would be entirely possible just to put some smooth curve through the actual values and make use of this to construct Earth-models at different stages of evolution. But a linear relation of the form (3) can obviously represent the data with such high accuracy that little if anything could be gained by any alternative procedure. Another advantage of adopting the linear form is that for any homogeneous region it implies a

TABLE 3

PHYSICAL PROPERTIES OF THE INTERIOR OF THE EARTH

Depth(km)	v_p(km/s)	v_s(km/s)	ρ(g/cm^3)	k(10^{12}cgs)	p(10^{12}cgs)
33	7.75	4.35	3.32	1.16	0.009
100	7.95	4.45	3.38	1.24	0.031
200	8.26	4.60	3.47	1.38	0.065
300	8.58	4.76	3.55	1.54	0.100
400	8.93	4.94	3.63	1.71	0.136
413	20°-DISCONTINUITY				
500	9.66	5.32	3.89	2.15	0.174
600	10.24	5.66	4.13	2.57	0.213
700	10.67	5.93	4.33	2.90	0.256
800	11.01	6.13	4.49	3.19	0.30
900	11.25	6.27	4.60	3.41	0.35
1000	11.43	6.36	4.68	3.59	0.39
1200	11.71	6.50	4.80	3.88	0.49
1400	11.99	6.62	4.91	4.20	0.58
1600	12.26	6.73	5.03	4.52	0.68
1800	12.53	6.83	5.13	4.87	0.78
2000	12.79	6.92	5.24	5.23	0.88
2200	13.03	7.02	5.34	5.57	0.99
2400	13.27	7.12	5.44	5.90	1.09
2600	13.50	7.21	5.54	6.23	1.20
2800	13.64	7.30	5.63	6.47	1.32
2898	13.64	7.30	5.68	6.51	1.37
2898	MANTLE-CORE BOUNDARY				
2898	8.10		9.43	6.2	1.37
3000	8.22		9.57	6.5	1.47
3200	8.47		9.85	7.1	1.67
3400	8.76		10.11	7.8	1.85
3600	9.04		10.35	8.5	2.04
3800	9.28		10.56	9.1	2.22
4000	9.51		10.76	9.7	2.40
4200	9.70		10.94	10.3	2.57
4400	9.88		11.11	10.8	2.73
4600	10.06		11.27	11.4	2.88
4800	10.26		11.41	12.0	3.03
4982	10.44		11.54	12.6	3.17
5121	9.7		14.20		3.27
5121	INNER-CORE BOUNDARY				
5121	11.16		16.80		3.27
5200	11.18		16.85		3.32
5400	11.21		16.96		3.42
5600	11.25		17.05		3.50
5800	11.27		17.12		3.56
6000	11.29		17.16		3.61
6200	11.30		17.19		3.63
6371	11.31		17.20		3.64

Fig. 1.

THE VALUES OF THE BULK-MODULUS k PLOTTED AGAINST THE PRESSURE p FOR THE EARTH

THE STRAIGHT LINES ARE k = a + 3·5 p FOR THE MANTLE AND CORE

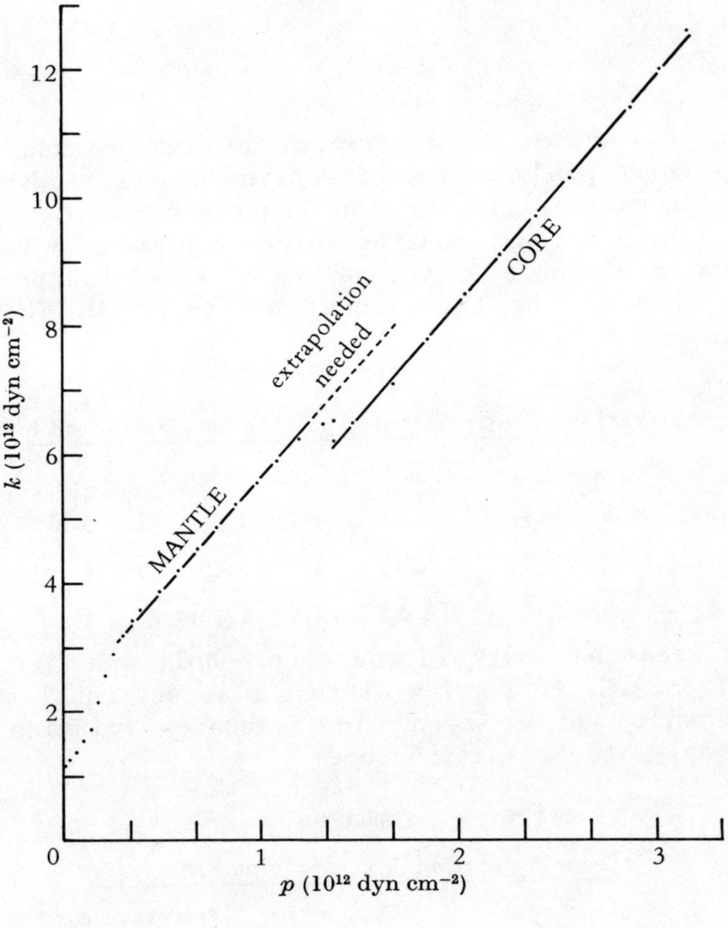

(Based on values taken from <u>The Earth as a Planet</u>, Ch. III, p.96, Chicago 1958).

simple analytical pressure-density relation. For in such a region

$$k \equiv \rho \frac{dp}{d\rho} = a + bp, \qquad \text{.... (4)}$$

by the definition of k in the theory of elasticity, and upon integration this yields

$$p = \frac{a}{b}\left\{\left(\frac{\rho}{\rho_u}\right)^b - 1\right\} \qquad \text{.... (5)}$$

wherein ρ_u arises as a constant of integration, and clearly corresponds to the effective uncompressed density of the material in the zone concerned.

By making a least-squares solution using the values of k and p of Table 3, the values of a and b appropriate to each of the three zones may be found. The results are as follows :

TABLE 4

Linearity of k against p : solving both for a and b

	$a(10^{12}$cgs)	b	Range of k	Mean-square differences of k
Outer shell (0-413 km)	1.11	4.35	1.16-1.71	0.01
Mantle (413-2898 km)	2.05	3.47	2.15-6.51	0.19
Liquid Core (2898-4982 km)	1.29	3.52	6.2-12.6	0.07

It is seen that only in the outer-shell does b differ much from 3.5. If in view of this b is set equal to 3.5 beforehand, and a second least-squares solution made for a only, the results become:

TABLE 5

Linearity of k with p : solving for a only

	$a(10^{12}$cgs)	b	Range of k	Mean-square differences of k
Outer shell	1.17	3.5	1.16-1.71	0.04
Mantle	2.03	3.5	2.15-6.51	0.19
Liquid core	1.34	3.5	6.2-12.6	0.07

The numerical values of Table 3 are given to no more than two decimal-places, and accuracy of the final digit is not claimed by Jeffreys & Bullen, while for the core the value of k is given to only one decimal-place. Thus even if a alone is solved for in the three zones (with b put equal to 3.5), the degree of fit is seen from Tables 4 and 5 to be almost equally good, as indicated by the mean-square differences of the resulting k-values which only show any change by as little as 0.01 to 0.04 for the outer shell.

Several models of the Earth have been computed by Bullen, Jeffreys, and others, and show the close linearity of behaviour of k against p in the three main zones. Such models have been constructed to be consistent with the Earth as a whole, where the total mass, radius, and moment-of-inertia, for example, are concerned, as well as satisfying the seismic data. Where considerations of later chapters of the present work are developed, the really important feature emerging at this stage is that the mantle-material has greater incompressibility k, at any relevant pressure, than has the core-material. This is shown by the values of **a** in the above Tables where for b = 3.5, k = 2.03 + 3.5 p (in units of 10^{12} dyn/cm^2) for the mantle, while k = 1.34 + 3.5p in the liquid core. For the solution in which b differs slightly from 3.5 in the two zones, the value of k is again always greater for the mantle than for the core for any pressure prevailing in the Earth, and in particular that at the core-mantle boundary. As will be demonstrated later, this feature is of the utmost importance, since it leads to the conclusion that for an Earth evolving by the gradual conversion of mantle-material to a different phase as core material, the greater compressibility of the latter (smaller k for given p) will cause the Earth to undergo contraction.

A pressure-density relation expressible analytically, such as the form (5), has the advantage that the theory of planetary structure can be developed mathematically, besides purely numerically, to show how the various parameters are related. For example, apart from a dimensionless numerical factor, the overall radius of a 1-zone planet satisfies the proportionality

$$r_s^2 \propto G^{-1}(b - 1)^{-1} a\rho_u^{-2} \qquad \ldots. (6)$$

where G is the constant of gravitation, and a, b, ρ_u as defined above. Other properties may similarly be expressed. As already noted, in obtaining the form (5) of the pressure-density relation from (4), the constant of integration leads to the introduction of ρ_u, the uncompressed density of the material. By using the values of ρ and p as given in Table 3, for each zone ρ_u can be found for each pair of (p,ρ)-values, since the quantities a and b are known, and the arithmetic-mean adopted as the relevant uncompressed density. The results are as follows:

TABLE 6

Outer shell	ρ_u	=	$3{\cdot}298 \pm 0{\cdot}006$ g/cm³
Mantle	ρ_u	=	$4{\cdot}057 \pm 0{\cdot}015$ g/cm³
Liquid core	ρ_u	=	$6.107 \pm 0{\cdot}004$ g/cm³

When calculations along the foregoing lines were first carried out in the early 1960's, the writer had in mind for the expected structure of the Earth the widely accepted notion that the core was constituted of iron, or iron and nickel, which owing to high density had gradually drained down from above, and it came as a complete surprise when the effective uncompressed density of the core-material turned out to be as low as 6.1 g/cm³ when that of iron is 7.8 g/cm³ in ordinary solid form and still rather greater than 7.0 g/cm³ when in molten form at standard pressure. For a time it was thought that there must be a mistake of arithmetic, but no amount of re-calculation could shake the result. Even if iron at the high pressures and temperature of the core were capable of existing in some different phase from ordinary molten iron at atmospheric pressure, it is difficult to suppose that any such phase would involve greater bulk (lower density) than when the pressure is released, which is what a figure of 6.1 g/cm^3 would require. It is the case that any such phase would not persist physically if the pressure were removed, but conceptually the uncompressed density here arrived at would refer to the material remaining in the same phase but at low pressure, just as, for example, a gas consisting of free protons and electrons in equal number, which physically requires high temperature, could be regarded conceptually as existing in that state at low ordinary temperatures and satisfying the gas-law with the same mean molecular weight as if it remained fully ionised, even though in an actual system the protons and electrons would combine to ordinary hydrogen.

Apart from an actual estimate by Ramsey of 4.8 g/cm^3 which will be referred to in a later chapter, an explicit value for the effective uncompressed density of the core-material does not seem to have been derived prior to the calculations upon which the foregoing value of 6.1 g/cm^3 was based, or at all events does not appear prominently in geophysical literature. More certainly, neither does any statement of the inescapable consequence of it, first pointed out by Ramsey, namely that the core cannot consist of iron. (Inclusion of a proportion of nickel, with its still higher density of 8.8 g/cm^3 in solid form and about 7.5 g/cm^3 when molten, could obviously in no way avert this conclusion that the core is not iron and nickel but only strengthen it). It might of course be possible to "save the situation" by watering the density down in a purely ad-hoc way, as for example by postulating a modicum of silicon (density 2.4 g/cm^3). But after it has been maintained for decades that the core is composed of iron and nickel, it is scarcely good science to make light-hearted addition of silicon or other light substance without at the same time showing where the evidence on which the earlier strongly held view had been based was not after all as reliable as it was claimed to be, as will be shewn in Chapter 5 to be the truth of the matter.

As a point of theoretical interest, it may be noted

that an effective uncompressed-density must exist at any level in the Earth, whether a linear relation between k and p holds or not, just as in a gaseous star there is an effective polytropic-index at every level whether the distribution is a polytrope or not. In the present case, if k, p, and ρ were known as a function of depth, the effective uncompressed density at any point may be shown to be given by

$$\rho_u = \rho\left\{1 - \frac{p}{k}\frac{dk}{dp}\right\}^{(dp/dk)} \quad .... \quad (7)$$

With a continuous series of values of k, p, ρ, use of this relation would yield a value of ρ_u at every depth in each zone. But the values arrived at would differ insignificantly from those already found above, and the procedure would not appreciably alter the value of 6.1 g/cm^3 for the uncompressed density of the liquid material in the core.

REFERENCES AND NOTES

Allen C.W. Astrophysical Quantities, 3rd edn, Athlone Press, 1973.

Bernal J.D. Observatory, 59, 268, 1936.

In this Bernal suggested that the 20°-discontinuity at depth 413 km represents a phase-change to a denser crystal form. Since the term "20°-discontinuity" is special to the Earth in its present form, and the discontinuity occurs in other planets, it will be simpler to refer to this as the "Bernal phase-change".

Bullen K. Introduction to the Theory of Seismology, 3rd edn, Cambridge, 1963.

Holmes A. The Age of the Earth, Nelson, 1937.

Holmes A. Principles of Physical Geology, Ronald Press, New York, 1945.

Jeffreys H. The Earth, 5th edn, Cambridge, 1970.

Lyttleton R.A. Comets and Their Origin, Cambridge,1953.

Lyttleton R.A. On the Phase-Change Hypothesis for the Structure of the Earth. Proc.Roy.Soc.A287, 471,1965.

Macdonald G.J.F. Journ.Geophys.Research, 64, 11, 1959.

Proceedings of the 7th & 8th Lunar Science Conferences, 3150, 1976, and 509, 1977.
These contributions report on the thermal gradients measured at points of the lunar surface, and their implication of high radioactive content as with the outer layers of the Earth.

Ramsey W.H. Geophys. Supplement : Mon.Not.Roy.Astron. Soc. 5, 409, 1949.

Shimazu Y. Journal of Earth Science, 2, 15, 1954.

3

The Nature of Tidal Friction

In a natural dynamical system, if there is relative motion of any of its parts, dissipation of energy will inevitably occur through frictional forces however slight. Evolution of the system will accompany this, and can result sometimes in sudden change to an entirely different configuration. The ultimate state will be such that all relative velocities have been reduced to zero. The type of friction here concerned is not static friction, as when a rough body rests on an inclined plane, but friction depending on the relative velocities and vanishing with them. The forces arising from such friction are linear functions of the velocities when these are small.

If a wheel is spinning on an axle, however nearly smooth, <u>some</u> dissipation of energy will occur until the wheel is brought to rest. A part of the energy may minutely heat and wear the bearing, and if the wheel is in contact with the air this too will provide another source of dissipation that will help to slow the rotation. If a flat circular plate were skimmed through empty space, its axis of rotation would at first undergo a conical motion and the plate appear to wobble, executing the so-called Eulerian nutation. This would bring about strains in the material, and unless the plate were perfectly rigid (which no actual material is), these strains would involve minute relative velocities within the plate as it bends slightly, and these in turn would result in dissipation of some of the energy of rotation. The lost kinetic energy would reappear as heating of the plate before being radiated away into space. However, no such internal forces can affect the total rotatory momentum of the system as a whole, though in a system of more than one component they can re-distribute it. In the present case the plate will finally come to rotate exactly in its own plane with the axis of rotation perpendicular to that plane and in the same direction as the original angular-momentum vector. All relative velocities within the plate will have come to vanish, and the state of lowest energy of the system consistent with the invariable angular momentum will have been reached. Only externally applied forces could now alter that configuration.

Where the Earth-Moon system is concerned, each body describes an orbit about their common centre-of-mass. Since the mass-ratio of the Earth to the Moon is 81.3 and the mean lunar distance is 3.8440×10^5 km, this centre-of-mass lies within the body of the Earth at mean distance 4671 km from its centre and therefore at about 1700 km below the surface. It is this centre-of-mass that describes the closely elliptical "orbit of the Earth" about the Sun, and not the centre of the Earth itself. Relative to the centre of the Earth, the Moon describes an exceedingly complicated path, and although much of this motion can be described by an ellipse of small mean-eccentricity (0.0549) and mean-inclination to the ecliptic (5° 9'), the complete motion also involves a great number of periodic perturbations produced mainly by the action of the Sun, together with quite small but very numerous terms from planetary action. Although these are all of high importance in the lunar theory itself, in the problem of tidal friction, where it is the cumulative effects of minute secular terms over extremely long periods of time that are concerned, these periodic terms average out, and it is permissible to assume the Moon to move uniformly about the Earth in a circular orbit, with the axis of rotation of the Earth perpendicular to this plane of orbital motion.

For almost the whole development of the dynamical lunar theory, the Sun, Earth, and Moon can be treated as point-masses, and if they were all perfectly symmetrical spherically, as the Sun seems to be within present measurable accuracy, they could always be so regarded, and the motion of the Moon calculated as if the Earth and Moon were point-masses at their centres. But in fact the Earth has finite size and is not perfectly rigid even at its solid parts ; moreover it is largely covered by deepish water which has no rigidity at all, other than when in the form of ice. The motion of the Moon is itself influenced by the feature that the gravitational potential of the Earth at external points is not solely that of a point-mass but contains a sizable second-order harmonic term resulting mainly from the oblateness of figure. The motions of artificial satellites, because of their close proximity to the Earth, are measurably affected by several other harmonic terms in its gravitational potential too.

To explain briefly the nature of tidal friction, let it be supposed to begin with that the body of the Earth is rigid and its surface regular but <u>entirely</u> covered to considerable depth by an ocean of water. (The oceans and seas amount to about 1/4000th of the mass of the Earth, and if spread uniformly over the whole surface would have a depth between 2 and 3 km.) The shape of the outer surface of this ocean would be determined by the attraction of the Moon, plus the centrifugal effect of the orbital motion about the centre-of-mass, which both vary with position and combine to subject the water to a tide-raising potential. If the Earth rotated at the same rate as would the Moon in a circular orbit, there would be a permanent distortion fixed relative to the Earth with the surface raised at the points H and H' (Fig.2) and lowered at points 90° away from these such as L and L'. The difference in level would be about 10^{-7} of the radius of the Earth or some 66 centimetres. But the Earth is in rotation more rapid than the Moon in its orbit, and even if the highest points H and H' were to remain directly in line with the Moon, the result would be a tidal wave progressing round the Earth in the opposite sense to its rotatory motion. The Sun also exerts a tide-raising force, but despite its far greater mass than that of the Moon, it is only about half as strong because of the much greater distance of the Sun, which enters as the inverse-cube. For this idealised Earth, the solar tide would have its greatest heights directly in line with the Sun, and produce a wave superposed on that of the lunar tide. In the open oceans on the actual Earth, the range of height of the combined tides averages about 75 centimetres.

But in fact the Earth rotates comparatively rapidly in relation to the orbital motions of the Moon and the Sun, and the tidal waves are carried forward ahead of the Moon and ahead of the Sun, as seen from the centre of the Earth. It is these displacements that are the source of tidal friction. The bulge of high-water nearer the Moon exerts a forward attraction upon it greater than the backward attraction of the more distant opposite bulge, and the former also acts at a larger angle to the line joining the centres of the bodies than does the latter, as may be seen from Fig.2. The net result integrated over the whole surface of the Earth is a force urging the Moon forward in its orbit. There must therefore be an exactly equal reaction on the water dragging it in the opposite sense to the rotation of the Earth trying to bring the bulges back directly under the Moon and Sun, and the drag will be communicated to the solid body of the Earth by viscosity to slow down its rotation. Some of the energy of rotation of the Earth will be dissipated to reappear as heat. The present rate of this dissipation, as will be shown later, is about 3.3×10^{19} erg per sec, whereas the rotatory kinetic energy of the Earth is about 2.14×10^{36} erg, showing that times of the order of 10^{9} years are involved in significant evolution of the rotation of the Earth and of the lunar orbit. The angular momentum intrinsic to the Earth is accordingly being reduced, but the <u>total</u> within the Earth-Moon system as a whole must be conserved, and in fact that lost by the Earth is transferred by the forward acting force on the Moon to its orbital motion, so that the Moon is gradually receding from the Earth ; the present rate is about

4 cm per year. (The rotatory momentum of the Moon itself is utterly negligible in the problem, but in any event since the Moon would continue to face the Earth in synchronous rotation this momentum would diminish to make a further minute contribution to that of the relative orbit.)

Now the actual Earth differs in many respects from the foregoing idealised system and is far more complicated. The solid body of the Earth is not perfectly rigid, and the total tidal potential distorts it slightly throughout to produce the so-called bodily tide. The solid surface rises and falls through a range of about 15 centimetres by lunar action, and augmented by solar action the range is about 23 cm. This bodily tide will also necessarily have an associated phase-lag, though the present consensus seems to be that it is negligibly small. But it certainly cannot be so for the Moon. The Earth, principally because of its greater mass, imposes a far larger bodily tide on the Moon, and its phase-lag must have been sufficient to have brought about the state in which the same face is always presented to the Earth, making it now a truly equilibrium-tide, and to constrain it to remain in that configuration.

In the wide-ranging deep oceans far from any coastal margins, the phase-lag of the tides most probably is quite small, but in shallow water tidal waves propagate more slowly, while the chance forms of coastlines and bays together with their resonance-effects can bring about enormous enhancement of the heights of tides, and mean ranges of about 15 metres occur at innumerable places. Perhaps more important still for strong tidal friction, it may happen that a tidal wave is forced to progress through channels or seas more or less in north-south or south-north directions, such as the Irish Sea and the Bering Strait, for which it is clear that the greatest elevation of tide cannot keep up angularly with the position of the Moon, and thus is compelled to contribute much more to the tidal couple than an otherwise comparable wave unconstrained in the open ocean. Winds and barometric pressure can also at times importantly increase the height of tides. Associated with these various tide-producing forces,

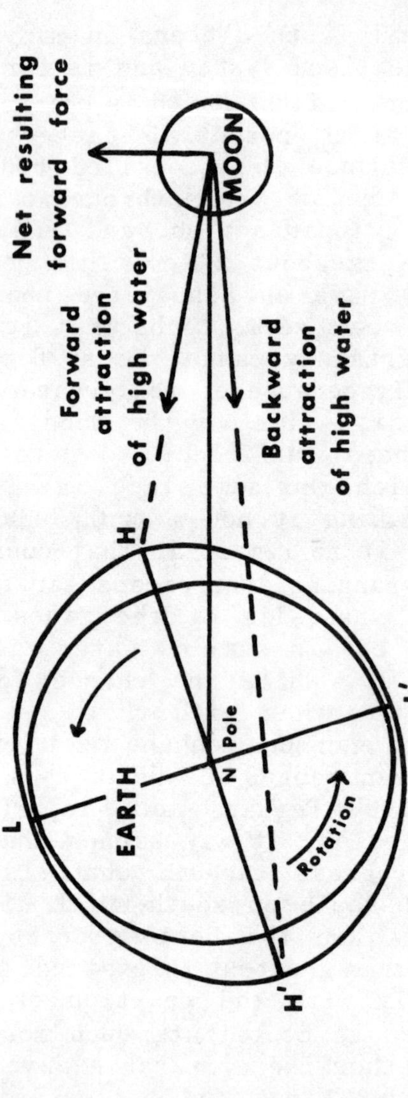
Net resulting forward force
MOON
Forward attraction of high water
Backward attraction of high water
H
L
L'
H'
EARTH
N Pole
Rotation

Fig. 2

and indeed with those acting on the terrestrial atmosphere (despite its having slightly less than one millionth of the whole Earth-mass), will be phase-lags to different degrees, not necessarily all in the same sense, and therefore generating corresponding tidal couples on the Earth. It is even possible that all the sources of tidal friction have not yet been recognised.

If the action of the Sun be left out of account for the present, the ultimate state of the Earth-Moon system as a result of tidal-friction dissipation must be such that no relative velocities remain between any of its elements, and this can only hold when the Earth has been brought to turn always the same face towards the Moon and they are both moving about each other in what may be termed rigid-body rotation in relative circular orbits, with the length of the "day" and of the "month" therefore equal. At the present time, the angular momentum carried in the Earth-Moon orbit is 4.87 times that of the rotation of the Earth. The former is proportional to $n^{-1/3}$, where $2\pi/n$ is the sidereal period in the lunar orbit, while the latter is proportional to the angular velocity ω of the Earth. Denoting the current values by n_0 and ω_0 respectively, (and assuming for present purposes that the moment-of-inertia of the Earth is not changing with time), conservation of angular momentum as the system evolves will require that

$$\frac{\omega}{\omega_0} + 4.87\left(\frac{n_0}{n}\right)^{1/3} = 5.87 \qquad \text{.... (1)}$$

It may readily be shown that if ω becomes equal to n, that is the day equal to the month, there are two possible solutions. For the first solution, the centre of the Moon would be rather less than 15,000 km from that of the Earth, and the rotation-period of the Earth and equal orbital period of the Moon round it as short as 4.9 hours. In the second solution, the distance of the Moon would be just over 1.44 times its value now (and so at nearly 555,000 km), while the corresponding equal lengths of the day and month would be just over 47 times the current length of the day.

It will emerge from later discussion herein that if the system evolved purely by tidal friction through sources operating today, and with the Moon starting slightly beyond the shorter-period distance (of about 15,000 km), this could have been only about 10^9 years ago, while the subsequent evolution to the 47-day period would require some 10^{11} years from now. However, if the Moon ever were at the proximity associated with the first solution of (1), the whole body of the satellite would in fact lie well within the so-called Roche limit for a small moon (here of density 3.3 g/cm^3) in orbital motion about a massive primary, the Earth (of greater mean-density 5.5 g/cm^3), and would as a result undergo enormous tidal distortion if not actual disruption into fragments sufficiently small to resist further tidal action by their internal cohesion. But there is almost inescapable evidence, reinforced by data from the recent landings on the Moon, that the lunar surface has undergone no major catastrophic event affecting the Moon as a whole for at least 4×10^9 years.

The rigid-body motion with period 47 days, should it ever be reached, would not in fact be the final state because of the action of solar tides not taken into account in the foregoing discussion. Since at this stage the Earth would still have rotation more rapid than its annual mean-motion round the Sun, solar tidal friction would act to slow its rotation, making the "day" very slightly longer than the "month". The situation as between the Earth and the Moon would now be reversed with the position of the Moon ahead of the tidal crest, and although subject to only minute frictional retardation the lunar tides would accelerate the rotation of the Earth with the necessary angular momentum supplied from the relative orbit, and thence transferred to the solar orbit, though affecting it utterly negligibly because of the great distance of the Sun compared with the Earth-Moon distance. As a result the Moon would now move in steadily towards the Earth, but it is quite impossible to make any estimate of the time taken for the Moon to reach the Earth beyond conjecturing that it could be a few orders of magnitude greater than the 10^{11} years or so needed for the

Moon to reach its greatest distance under purely tidal forces.

It would obviously be of considerable importance to the problem of the evolution of the lunar orbit if the amount of tidal friction occurring could be calculated directly and accurately from considerations of the physical properties of the seas and oceans, of the body of the Earth, and of the atmosphere. For the last of these, the couple arising from the thermal tide, which is produced by solar heating of the atmosphere, can in fact be found by means of meteorological measures of the resulting pressure-distribution over the globe, and while not entirely negligible turns out to make the least important contribution. Where the other possible sources are concerned, there can be little doubt that the seas and oceans contribute substantially to the energy-dissipation (though as yet the precise mechanisms are by no means agreed on), but the extent of the contribution of the solid Earth remains unsettled. The whole subject is fraught with great uncertainty owing to the irregular topography of ocean-basins and coastal margins, but even so what appear to be hopeful methods of attack on the problem have been developed in quite recent times on the basis of various models for the oceans (Lambeck, 1977). But none of the discussions envisages the possibility of a changing moment-of-inertia of the Earth, which will be shown later to be of prime importance to the whole problem.

Yet another potential source of information on the lengths of both the day and month in past ages may result from analysis of the growth-rhythms of corals and other organic structures that are subject to influence by annual, lunar, and diurnal periods. Investigations of the data involve considerable difficulties and many sources of uncertainty, but if secure results emerge, they could well supply valuable information enabling conclusions to extend much further back in time than those from presently available eclipse-data, and by several orders of magnitude. Again, the discussions so far attempted seem to have omitted to take into account the possibility of a changing moment-of-inertia of the Earth, but detailed consideration of these highly interesting questions would mean digressing too far from the main implications of the ancient eclipse-data. Accounts of recent work on both the direct calculation of tidal dissipation and analysis of coral-rhythms may be found in a volume of highest interest edited by Brosche & Sundermann (1978).

The prospect of making progress with the problem would be much restricted were there no other relevant phenomena, but an entirely different approach, though one not settling the precise source or mechanism of tidal friction, may be made from the circumstance that total eclipses of the Sun by the Moon take place. By a truly fortunate dispensation, the angular diameter of the Moon as seen from the Earth slightly exceeds that of the Sun during about 30 per cent of the year, though in varying amount. For the Moon, the mean diameter of about 31'.4 ranges by nearly 2' on either side of this owing to the non-circularity of the orbit, while the mean for the Sun is about 32'.0 with a range of only about ±0'.5 resulting from the present eccentricity (0.0167) of the relative orbit. Also the inclination of the lunar orbit is small enough for the Moon to interpose more or less directly between the Earth and the Sun fairly frequently. At least two eclipses of the Sun of some kind occur somewhere on Earth every year, and, though extremely rarely, as many as five : however, in by no means all of these is the Sun totally obscured from sight by the disc of the Moon, but in any century there are about sixty to seventy <u>total</u> eclipses. The comparatively narrow path of totality, averaging perhaps 100 km in breadth for different eclipses, produced by the moving shadow of the Moon, can fall almost anywhere on the surface of the (rotating) Earth, and it is remarkable how, although sometimes thousands of kilometres long, the limited strip of totality may miss almost all land-areas, never mind populous zones, requiring for their observation eclipse expeditions to remote parts of the globe. It is estimated that, at any given place on Earth, a total eclipse occurs on average about once every 360 years, and a high proportion of people may go through life without ever being privileged to observe one.

A total eclipse is so impressive a phenomenon, that many unmistakable accounts of such events have been found in the writings of the ancients, describing mysterious events that no doubt inspired much awe in superstitious witnesses, to some of whom it even seemed that "a fearful wolf was devouring the precious lamb" to leave them in perpetual darkness. Immediately prior to a total eclipse there is a gradual darkening of the sky for several minutes, the remaining sunlight taking on a strange hue, the temperature falls, and the shadow of the Moon may be seen advancing over the ground with great swiftness (some 2,000 km an hour or more) as if a heavy thunderstorm were approaching, but the final onset of darkness is very sudden as the first moment of totality is reached. The normally quite invisible solar corona flashes out as a brilliant halo extending

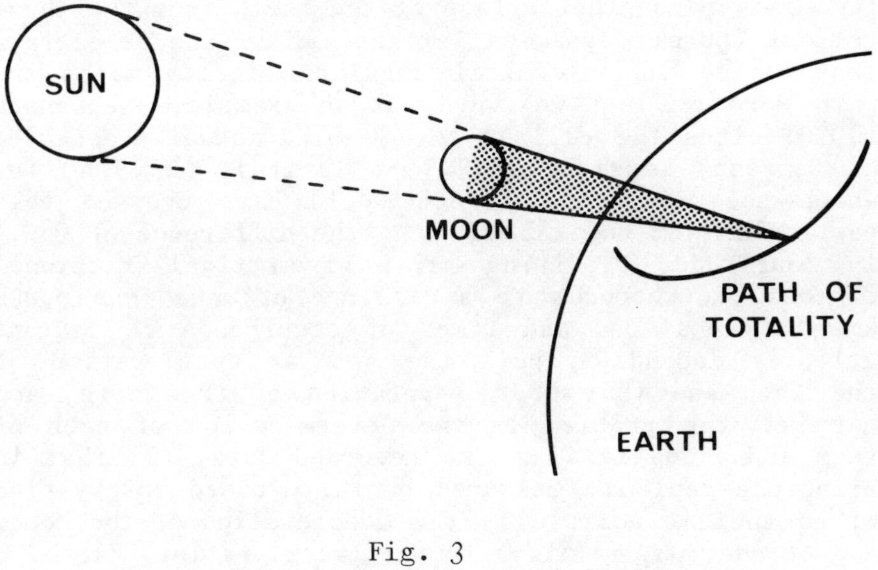

Fig. 3
Schematic drawing of a total eclipse.

to 10 or 20 solar radii, and brighter stars and planets become visible to the unaided eye. On a few occasions a comet has been easily seen that otherwise would have entirely escaped observation. These are only some of the associated phenomena, but the essential importance for our present purpose of any adequate record of an eclipse is that it will reveal that, as viewed from a known place on Earth and at a certain date, the Moon and the Sun had the same angular position in the sky.

Now it has been seen in a general way that tidal friction produces a small transverse force on the Moon urging it forward, and necessarily also a reaction-couple on the Earth braking its rotation. The forwards force, by adding angular momentum to the lunar orbit, in fact results in retarding the position of the Moon in its orbit, and thus, as compared with purely dynamical expectations, leads to delay in the time of occurrence of an eclipse of the Sun, while the slowing of the rotation of the Earth will bring about displacement of the path-of-totality on the surface traced by the moving shadow of the Moon. The latter in general has much the greater influence and moves the path of totality eastward on the surface of the Earth from the theoretical (purely dynamical) track, while the deceleration of the lunar orbital angular velocity moves the path more or less westward. As an example, Stephenson (1979) cites the eclipse of 136 B.C. actually observed at Babylon, longitude 44°.5 E, latitude 32°.5 N, for which the theoretical track would have crossed this particular latitude at 24° W : the difference of 68°.5 in longitude, resulting mainly from tidal-frictional effects, corresponds to a distance of more than 6,000 km. The locations and times of occurrence of ancient eclipses depend on both the secular acceleration of the Moon and that of the rotation of the Earth, and part of the problem is the determination of each of them individually from the recorded data. All that in principle could be measured by Earth-based observation of an ancient eclipse is the acceleration of the Moon, and of the Sun, relative to the (accelerating) Earth.

It will later appear that the magnitude of this force on the Moon is less than one million-millionth

$(1/10^{12})$ of the attractive force exerted on it by the Earth, which suggests that considerable periods of time are likely to be needed for noticeable effect on the position of the Moon to build up. It is for this reason that ancient eclipses are all-important. However, it is clear that before any use can be made of ancient-eclipse data, it is necessary to know as accurately as possible where the Moon would have been if there were no tidal friction acting. This is the province of lunar theory, which is that branch of dynamical astronomy concerned with the motion of the Moon under purely gravitational forces. When a scientific theory is first put forward, the extent to which it can explain and correlate a range of phenomena, and especially its power to make successful predictions (here the position of the Moon at any time), are what constitute its triumphs. But later, when the theory has become well established and regarded as highly reliable, it is its failures to give acceptably correct results that may become in a sense its even greater successes. For such failures may mean that something new is also involved, that some feature of the problem has not yet been appreciated, that some unrecognised process may be at work, with the theory not quite right despite its former successes. The discovery of any such new processes is of course one of the main objects of scientific theory and experiment.

The paradigm and exemplar of scientific theories remains the dynamical theory of newtonian gravitation. Considerable mathematical difficulties were associated with the working out of its consequences to a stage where results competed in accuracy with observations, but some 150 years were to go by before it appeared to be showing signs of failure when the motion of the planet Uranus, discovered in 1781, seemed increasingly to fail to conform to predictions on the inverse-square law. There was perhaps a good deal more disputation about this particular difficulty than was really warranted, and suffice to recall here that it was eventually cleared up without need for any adjustment of the theory itself by the discovery in 1846 of the planet Neptune, the gravitational effect of which was the unrecognised factor behind the apparent failure. Everything seemed then to be back in good order with the theory. But the period of relaxation proved to be fairly shortlived, for soon a difficulty arose with the motion of the perihelion of Mercury, which has a highly eccentric orbit by planetary standards and therefore a well-defined perihelion, and this was shown in 1859 by LeVerrier to be getting progressively out of position by some 40" (seconds of arc) per century, a large angle where planets are concerned. It may be worth noting that such a phenomenon could never be discovered without the existing theory : no amount of mere observing of Mercury could disclose the anomaly. For several decades, explanation resisted all attempts by means of standard hypotheses, but as is now well known the problem was satisfactorily resolved only with the advent of the general theory of relativity, which implied that for a planet moving so near the Sun slight modifications of the newtonian laws were needed.

While these difficulties were being encountered in the planetary theory, further trouble arose from curious increasing deviation of the position of the Moon from the predictions of the lunar theory. The problem had its beginnings long before through work by Halley who in 1695, from studies of then-known ancient eclipses, concluded that there must be an acceleration of the Moon in its orbit round the Earth. This was to remain an acute difficulty for a long time to come, the more so when the renowned Euler proved in 1770 that there was no possible defect in the lunar theory itself that could accommodate such an acceleration. But then in 1786 Laplace showed that an extremely minute long-term rate of decrease was taking place in the eccentricity e' of the orbit of the Sun about the Earth-Moon system (it is actually an oscillation of exceptionally long period of the order of 10^5 years), and although unimportant where short-term planetary predictions are concerned, nevertheless exerts an unexpectedly large indirect effect on the motion of the Moon. The numerical effect calculated by Laplace seemed to account for the whole existing discrepancy with all-sufficient accuracy. There the matter rested for many years, theory apparently agreeing closely with observation, until J.C.Adams, of Neptune fame, looked into the question again in 1853 with much greater thoroughness. He found that investigation only to the first order, as given by Laplace, was quite inadequate for the reason that higher-order terms which a priori had been tacitly assumed to be negligible, when actually calculated turned out to have extraordinarily large numerical coefficients, and their inclusion reduced the theoretical effect to only about half the observed amount. Despite the incontrovertible nature of the mathematical treatment given by Adams, his belated discovery and overthrow of a long-unquestioned result excited widespread controversy and even disbelief on the grounds that it conflicted with observation, before being accepted as correct. The whole affair is one of historic scientific interest, but suffice it here to say that the importance of this work by Adams cannot be over-emphasised for its value in establishing for certain that some unrecognised influence was perturbing the motion of the Moon. Thus was ushered in the theory of tidal friction.

In the lunar theory, the longitude v of the Moon can be proved to be expressible in the form

$$v(\text{longitude}) = nt + \varepsilon + \text{periodic terms} + \left[\tfrac{1}{2}\dot{n}t^2\right] \quad ,..(1)$$

wherein n denotes the mean angular motion, so that $2\pi/n$ is the period in the lunar orbit (the sidereal month), ε is a constant associated with the instant from which t is chosen to be measured, but without the final term $\frac{1}{2}\dot{n}t^2$ shown in the square-brackets. But after the correct allowance had been made for the effect of the slowly changing solar eccentricity e', the longitude of the Moon was found no longer to conform to purely dynamical theory, and there reappeared on the scene this unexplained term proportional to t^2. The quantity $\dot{n}$ represents an (angular) acceleration of the Moon, now attributed to tidal friction. The trigonometrical periodic terms in (1), although of considerable importance and accurately calculable in the lunar theory itself, average out to zero over long periods of time, and thus produce no steadily increasing (or decreasing) secular effects, as however the term in t^2 does.

Reaching ahead for the moment, the acceleration $\dot{n}$ here concerned is found to be negative, as already noted, and its numerical value as determined by different methods comes to about -30" per century per century (it is an acceleration of an angular velocity and there fore of dimensions $TIME^{-2}$) In one year it would cause the observed longitude of the Moon to differ from the theoretical longitude by only 0".0015, but in 1,000 years the difference would amount to nearly $0^{\circ}.5$, while for the very earliest record so far known of an eclipse observed at Ugarit in what is now Syria on 3rd May, 1375 B.C., the difference would be nearly 5°.

Analysis of the ancient-eclipse data has been further complicated down the years in another way by the circumstance that, whereas the equations of dynamical astronomy automatically assume that the time involved must be true dynamical time, observations were always necessarily made against the rotating Earth as timekeeper until comparatively recent years. Observations accumulated over a century or more, however, had gradually disclosed that the Sun as seen from the Earth, and the planets Mercury and Venus (regarded as seen from the Sun), all suffered from unexplained secular accelerations in their longitudes, and in amount precisely in proportion with their orbital mean-motions. As the outcome of a meticulous analysis by H.S. Jones (1939), it was eventually shown that all these discrepancies could be simultaneously removed by the single hypothesis that the rate of rotation of the Earth was undergoing a steady retardation, and that they had therefore arisen from the tacit unrecognised assumption that the Earth could be regarded as an astronomical clock keeping true dynamical time. A spurious acceleration from the same source must therefore in part have been influencing the measured position of the Moon against the rotation of the Earth as timekeeper. But with this pseudo-acceleration known from the solar and planetary orbits, it could appropriately be allowed for in the lunar theory, and this finally enabled the longitude of the Moon to be expressed in terms of true dynamical time, always supposing that the constant of gravitation itself is not varying. The angular velocity of the Earth is also subject to minute seasonal and irregular fluctuations together with unexplained infinitesimal nutations, which although raising important problems are not considered relevant to tidal-friction theory.

For these reasons, time measured by the rotating Earth came to be replaced in recent years by so-called ephemeris-time, which is defined by means of the orbit of the Earth (the centre-of-mass of the Earth-Moon system) about the Sun. But once again, this might not turn out to be true dynamical time if G were changing, as some recent cosmologies seriously propose. If G were decreasing, it would result in a general increase of all orbital distances in the solar system accompanied by correspondingly increasing periods, in particular the length of the year. Many years of radar-ranging to the planets will probably be needed to detect the rate of change of G claimed by the various theories, but lunar laser-ranging may well settle the question somewhat sooner. Still more recently, there has been introduced a third standard of time known as atomic-time which is measured by means of a highly stable caesium-resonator, an apparatus believed to yield true dynamical time. The strict definitions of these several time-standards and the relations between them (with comprehensive source-references are to be found in Allen (1973 : Ch.2 references).

With the foregoing brief description of the general nature of tidal friction and of the lengthy background leading stage by stage to the recognition of the occurrence of tidal friction, it is proposed next to consider the dynamical theory by which the ancient-eclipse data may be analysed and interpreted.

REFERENCES AND NOTES

Adams J.C. On the Secular Variation of the Moon's Mean-motion, Phil.Trans.Roy.Soc. 143, 397, 1853.

Adams J.C. Collected Scientific Papers, Vol.I, xxxv et seq., Cambridge, 1896.

This contains a detailed account of the lengthy controversy that ensued from Adams's correction of Laplace's theory.

Brosche P. & Sundemann J. (Editors), Tidal Friction and the Earth's Rotation, Springer-Verlag, Berlin, 1978.

Euler L. Academy Prize, 9, French Academy, 1770.

Halley E. Phil. Trans. Roy. Soc. 19, 160, 1695.

Jeffreys H. The Earth, edns 1-6, Cambridge, 1924-1976.

Jones H.S. The Rotation of the Earth and Secular Accelerations of Sun, Moon, and Planets, Mon. Not. Roy. Astron. Soc. 99, 541, 1939.

Lambeck K. Tidal Dissipation in the Oceans, Phil.Trans. Roy. Soc. A 287, 545, 1977.

The equations of motion are questionable in that they do not contemplate a changing moment-of-inertia.

LeVerrier U.J.J. Annals of Paris Observatory, t.V, Ch. XV, 75 et seq., 1859.

Laplace P.S. Memoirs of the French Academy, 1786.

Lyttleton R.A. The Stability of Rotating Liquid Masses, Cambridge, 1953.

The nature of secular stability for rotating systems is defined and its distinction from ordinary stability demonstrated.

Stephenson F.R. A Modern Look at Ancient Eclipses, New Scientist, 22 Feb 1979.

4

The Theory of Tidal Friction

It is standard procedure in relating the effects of tidal friction to the apparent secular accelerations of the Moon and Sun derived from observations to regard the lunar orbit as circular at all stages and the rotation vector of the Earth as perpendicular to this plane of motion. The orbit of the Sun relative to the centre-of-mass of the Earth-Moon system is also assumed to be circular with the Sun moving uniformly in it. The following usual notation will be adopted, with the numerical values taken from Allen C.W., Astrophysical Quantities, 1973.

M = mass of the Earth = 5.976×10^{27} g,

m = mass of the Moon = 7.350×10^{25} g,

m' = mass of the Sun = 1.989×10^{33} g,

ω = angular velocity of the Earth = 7.292×10^{-5} per sec.,

C = moment-of-inertia of the Earth about polar axis = 8.04×10^{44} cm^2 g,

c = mean Earth-Moon distance = 3.8440×10^{10} cm,

n = mean-motion of Moon in relative orbit = 2.662×10^{-6} per sec.,

c' = semi-major axis of solar orbit = 1.496×10^{13} cm,

n' = mean-motion of the Sun in orbit = 1.991×10^{-7} per sec.,

G = constant of gravitation = 6.668×10^{-8} cgs.

These are the present values, but in the sequel the same symbols will be used to denote values of ω, C, c, and n changing with time, and when distinction needs to be made, present values will be denoted by ω_o, C_o, c_o, and n_o.

As explained in the previous chapter, it is the angular positions of the Moon and Sun relative to a meridian on the Earth itself undergoing acceleration of its rotation that can be determined from observations, and these yield their apparent secular accelerations ν and ν', which when expressed in terms of $\dot{n}$, $\dot{n}'$, and $\dot{\omega}$ are as follows:

$$\left.\begin{aligned} \nu &= \dot{n} - \frac{n}{\omega}\dot{\omega}, \\ \nu' &= \dot{n}' - \frac{n'}{\omega}\dot{\omega}. \end{aligned}\right\} \quad \ldots. \; (1)$$

If both n and ω are changing, the apparent displacement of the moon in longitude in sidereal time T is through an angle $\frac{1}{2}\nu T^2$, and similarly for the Sun is $\frac{1}{2}\nu' T^2$.

At any stage of their evolution through tidal effects, the lunar and solar orbits will satisfy respectively the relations

$$n^2 c^3 = G(M + m), \quad n'^2 c'^3 = G(m' + M + m) \quad \ldots. \; (2)$$

When the values are changing with time, it is convenient to replace c and n by a single variable ξ, thus

$$c = c_o \xi^2, \qquad n = n_o \xi^{-3} \qquad \ldots. \; (3)$$

and similarly for the values of the Sun, introducing a parameter ξ',

$$c' = c'_o \xi'^2, \qquad n' = n'_o \xi'^{-3}, \qquad \ldots. \; (4)$$

so that equations (2) are automatically satisfied at every stage, the suffix o indicating the present values as aforesaid.

The angular momentum h in the orbital motion of the Earth-Moon system about the common centre-of-mass is given by

$$h = Mmc^2n/(M + m) = Mmc_o{}^2n_o\xi/(M + m), \qquad ....(5)$$

and there is a similar expression for that of the Sun about the Earth-Moon system. Hence if -N is the total tidal couple produced by the Moon on the Earth, a couple +N will act on the Moon in its relative orbit, and accordingly

$$\frac{Mmc_o{}^2n_o}{M + m}\ \frac{d\xi}{dt} = N. \qquad .... (6)$$

Since the mass of the Moon is negligible compared with that of the Earth and Sun, if -N' is the total couple, tidal plus thermal, on the Earth produced by the Sun, the corresponding equation is

$$\frac{m'Mc_o'^2n_o}{m' + M}\ \frac{d\xi'}{dt} = N' . \qquad .... (7)$$

These are well-known standard equations in the form and notation given by Jeffreys in successive editions of The Earth.

In view of (3) & (4), these equations for $\dot{\xi}$ and $\dot{\xi}'$ immediately yield $\dot{n}$ and $\dot{n}'$, but the expressions (1) for ν and ν' also involve $\dot{\omega}$, and to obtain this the effect of the couples -N and -N' on the rotation of the Earth is required. Since the angular momentum of the Earth is $C\omega$, the appropriate equation of motion is

$$\frac{d}{dt}(C\omega) = -N - N' . \qquad .... (8)$$

It is worth noting that this involves an important departure from all previous presentations of the theory in which the left-hand side of the equation has hitherto always been taken as

$$C\frac{d\omega}{dt},$$

which clearly could only be correct if C were constant.

But there can be no a-priori reason for supposing this, and indeed adoption of this incorrect form has only led to difficulties with the theory, as might well be expected. To discuss the point a little further : in the case of rotatory momentum, even if no couples act upon a body possessing angular momentum, its angular velocity will change if the moment-of-inertia should change. This will occur in accordance with

$$\frac{d}{dt}(C\omega) = 0, \qquad \text{.... (9)}$$

and if $\dot{C}$ is non-zero, an intrinsic angular acceleration $\dot{\omega}_i$ will result given by

$$C\frac{d\omega}{dt} = C\dot{\omega}_i = -\omega\dot{C} \qquad \text{....(10)}$$

Thus the rotation will change as if a fictitious couple $-\omega\dot{C}$ were acting on a body of moment-of-inertia C. Accordingly the correct equation for the total value of $\dot{\omega}$ including allowance for the lunar and solar couples is

$$C\frac{d\omega}{dt} = -N - (N' + \omega\dot{C}). \qquad \text{... (11)}$$

The importance to the theory of this amended form of the equation for $\dot{\omega}$ cannot be overemphasised. The final term $N' + \omega\dot{C}$ has been written in brackets in equation (11) since it will be found that in subsequent equations the two terms N' and $\omega\dot{C}$ always appear together as a sum in this way.

It is now possible, using (11), to express ν and ν' in terms of the couples N and N', as follows

$$\nu = -\frac{3\xi^{-4}(M + m)}{Mmc_o^2} N + \frac{n_o\xi^{-3}}{\omega C}(N + N' + \omega\dot{C}), \quad \ldots (12)$$

$$\nu' = -\frac{3\xi'^{-4}(m' + M)}{m'Mc'^2} N' + \frac{n'_o\xi'^{-3}}{\omega C}(N + N' + \omega\dot{C}). \quad \ldots (13)$$

It will emerge later that the ratio $3N'/(N + N' + \omega\dot{C})$ lies between about 0.3 and 0.4, while over the period of a few thousand years for which records of ancient eclipses extend, the values of ξ and ξ' will change negligibly from 1, and also the values of ω, C, and c differ only minutely from the present values. In these circumstances, the ratio of the first term in N' on the right in (13) to the second term in $N + N' + \omega\dot{C}$ is of order only 10^{-7}, and therefore quite negligible in the problem. This simply means that $\dot{n}'$ itself is vanishingly small, and that any measured apparent acceleration of the Sun can arise only from the part of ν' involving the acceleration $\dot{\omega}$ of the Earth, which will yield the value of $\dot{\omega}$ at once within the accuracy of determination of ν and ν'. The reason for this is that the changes of angular momentum resulting from the action of the Sun on the Earth are so minute compared with the angular momentum in the solar orbit itself that the latter undergoes entirely negligible change through the action of the couple N'. In fact the angular momentum in the Sun-Earth orbit is almost 10^6 times that in the Earth-Moon orbit, while N' is less than N though of comparable magnitude, as will later be shown.

The equations for ν and ν' can now be written with greater brevity by introducing the number κ defined by

$$\kappa = Mmc_0^2 n_0 / \{(M + m)C\omega\} = 4.87 \qquad .... (14)$$

which is the ratio of the present angular momentum in the Earth-Moon relative orbit, given by (5), to the present rotatory momentum of the Earth, the numerical value of which is readily found to be 4.87 as indicated. Then, if applied only for periods of no more than a few thousand years, it is permissible with all sufficient accuracy retained to put $\xi = \xi' = 1$ in (13) and (14), and to let ω, C, and c be given their current values. The equations for ν and ν' then take the form

$$\nu = \frac{M + m}{Mmc^2}\{(\kappa - 3)N + \kappa N'\} + n\frac{\dot{C}}{C}, \qquad .... (15)$$

$$\nu' = \frac{M + m}{Mmc^2}(\kappa N + \kappa N') + n'\frac{\dot{C}}{C}. \qquad .... (16)$$

In order to make use of these theoretical relations, numerical values of ν and ν' are next needed. A thorough rediscussion of all available ancient-eclipse data has in recent years been carried out by Stephenson and his collaborators, and the values arrived at supersede those of all earlier work. After setting up stringent conditions for standards of acceptability, they found some fifty records of such eclipses to be reliably satisfactory, and from these they have derived the following numerical values of ν and ν' with the associated standard-errors shown :

$$\nu = 12''.10 \pm 0''.34 \text{ per century}^2,$$

$$\nu' = 2''.94 \pm 0''.16 \text{ per century}^2. \qquad .... (17)$$

Upon multiplying (15) and (16) through by $C\omega/n$ and $C\omega/n'$ respectively, and converting to cgs-units, they are readily found to yield the following pair of equations

$$(1 - 3/\kappa)N + (N' + \omega\dot{C}) = (1.298 \pm 0.037) \times 10^{23}, \quad \ldots(18)$$

$$N + (N' + \omega\dot{C}) = (4.214 \pm 0.229) \times 10^{23}. \quad \ldots(19)$$

These equations, together with (24) below, imply that the couples N and N', with the fictitious couple $-\omega\dot{C}$, are all of general order 10^{23} cgs, and this is a standard unit for the various couples involved in the problem, as will be seen in the sequel. It is of special interest that the equations are effectively in only two independent variables, namely the lunar couple N on its own as one, and the sum $N'+\omega\dot{C}$ as the other. Remarkably enough, therefore, N can be uniquely determined from given values of ν and ν' even if C is changing with time (and G also, as will be seen subsequently in Chapter 9).

But the solar couple N' cannot be isolated on this information alone, and further considerations need to be introduced to achieve this when it is recognised that C may be changing, as it will be shown shortly that it must be.

On solution of (18) and (19), the value of N for the past 3350 years (over which eclipse-records extend) is readily found to be

$$N = (4.74 \pm 0.38) \times 10^{23} \text{ cgs.} \quad \ldots\ (20)$$

The corresponding value of $\dot{n}$ follows at once, using (3) and (6) with $\xi = 1$, as

$$\dot{n} = -\frac{3(M + m)}{Mmcn} N = -27''.2 \pm 2''.2 \text{ century}^{-2} \quad \ldots\ (21)$$

when expressed in the customary unit of seconds of arc per century-squared. The rate of recession of the Moon also follows, by using (3) and (6), to give

$$\dot{c} = \frac{2(M + m)}{Mmcn} N = 4.02 \pm 0.32 \text{ cm/year.} \quad .... (22)$$

Thus since the time of the earliest recorded eclipse, the Moon has receded from the Earth by about 0.135 km.

Before proceeding, it is of some interest to compare these results with other determinations of $\dot{n}$ and $\dot{c}$ based on different data and methods. The following values are given in a recent paper by Williams J.G., Sinclair W.S., and Yoder C.F. (Geophysical Research Letters, Vol. 5 No. 11, 943, 1978) :

TABLE 7

$\dot{n}$	$''/(cy)^2$	Authors
-22.4	± 4	Spencer Jones (1939)
-38.0	± 8	Oesterwinter & Cohen (1972)
-26.0	± 2	Morrison & Ward (1975)
-36.0	± 5	Van Flandern (1978)
-30.0	± 3	Muller (1976)
-24.6	± 5	Calame & Mulholland (1978)
-23.8	± 4	Williams, Sinclair & Yodel (1978)

The mean of these, weighted inversely as their errors, is $(-27.7 \pm 4.8)''/cy^2$, which agrees almost surprisingly well with (21). The second numerically least value in the above list, that derived by Williams et al., is based on data obtained over about eight years by lunar laser-ranging, and it implies a rate of recession of the Moon by 3.5 ± 0.6 cm per year, in good agreement with the present result (22). The value of $\dot{n}$ obtained by Morrison & Ward is based on observations of transits of Mercury during the past 300 years, and these yield a value of $\dot{c}$ of 3.8 ± 0.3 cm/yr, again closely according with (22) within the error-limits.

The foregoing results enable the past history of the lunar orbit through the influence of tidal friction to be examined. According to Jeffreys (loc. cit.), the formula for the lunar couple N, as calculated on equilibrium tidal theory, is given by

$$N = \frac{8\pi}{5} \cdot \frac{Gmr_S^4}{c^3} \rho H \sin 2\varepsilon, \qquad \ldots . \; (23)$$

where r_S is the surface-radius of the Earth, ρ the density of the tidally disturbed material, H the height of the tide, and ε the phase-lag angle. The couple N' on equilibrium theory will be given by an exactly similar expression involving m', c', and H'. If it is supposed that H is linearly proportional to the tide-raising potential, which depends on m/c^3 for the Moon and on m'/c'^3 for the Sun, then the ratio N/N' would be proportional to $(mc'^3/m'c^3)^2$ which is readily calculable and gives, for equilibrium tidal theory,

$$\frac{N}{N'} = 4.744. \qquad \ldots . \; (24)$$

Thus with N already known, its value (20) now enables the equilibrium tidal value of N'(tidal) to be found using (24), which yields $N' = (1.00 \pm 0.08) \times 10^{23}$ cgs. For non-linear (quadratic) friction, the ratio is more difficult of evaluation, but it has been shown by R.R. Newton that the corresponding ratio is somewhat reduced to N/N' = 3.8 approximately, so that in this case N'(tidal) $= (1.25 \pm 0.10) \times 10^{23}$ cgs.

For the past action of the Moon alone, the value of N will change in proportion to c^{-6}, so that $N = N_O(c_O/c)^6 = N_O\xi^{-12}$, where N_O is the present value, always assuming that the phase-angle is independent of the height of the tide. On this basis, equation (6) becomes

$$\frac{Mmc_o^2 n_o}{M + m} \cdot \frac{d\xi}{dt} = N_o \xi^{-12}, \qquad \ldots . \; (25)$$

and, taking the present time as corresponding to t = 0, this integrates to give

$$t = \frac{Mm\, c_o^2 n_o}{13(M + m)N_o}(\xi^{13} - 1). \qquad \ldots.(26)$$

The tidal couple obviously increases strongly with diminishing c or ξ, and for $\xi = \frac{1}{2}$, or $c = \frac{1}{4}c_o$, the term ξ^{13} is about 10^{-4} and quite negligible in view of other much greater uncertainties. Thus with N_o given by (20), the time at which the Moon would have been close to the Earth would have been at approximately $t = 1.5 \times 10^9$ years ago, which means less than half of the age of the known oldest rocks, considered to be a lower limit to the age of the Earth itself. Embarrassingly short as this resulting time-interval is, it could well be an overestimate for a number of reasons. As seen from (23), the couple N depends on $r_s{}^4H$, where r_s is the radius of the Earth, and H the height of the equilibrium-tide. Now H must be proportional at least to the strength of the tide raising potential, and so at least to the second power of r_s. Also, it will be shown later that $\dot{C}$ must be negative, which in turn implies a contracting Earth and hence that r_s in the past would have been greater than at present. When account is taken of this factor, the time for the close proximity of the Moon to the Earth on the present basis can be shown to have been only a little more than 10^9 years ago, and the time-scale difficulty rendered even more acute. (Lyttleton 1976 ; Lyttleton & Fitch 1978).

However, it must be remembered that the value of N given by (20) represents only an average based on eclipse-data distributed over some 3300 years, and in the absence as yet of earlier records, extrapolation to remote times measured in aeons assumes that N can always be given by the form (23) despite the considerable uncertainties involved. A changing surface-radius would be most likely to be accompanied by changes of surface-topography and coast-lines, with changes in depths of oceans and seas, all of which would be concerned in determining the total lunar couple and the solar tidal couple. Even the terrestrial atmosphere may have steadily changed in its properties, and thus mean changes in the fairly small (at present) though non-negligible thermal tidal couple arising from solar heating, which source of energy may not itself have remained precisely constant over aeons of time, if the ice-ages are anything to go by.

Even so, this short time under present assumptions at which the Moon would have been extremely close to the Earth does raise the interesting question whether other non-terrestrial influences may have acted on the lunar orbit to render the basis of the foregoing result too narrow. Comparatively recent capture of the Moon from an independent orbit as a planet seems to be entirely ruled out, for this could only come about dynamically, within less than an aeon ago, through the combined gravitational influence of the Sun and Earth, and this can be shown would involve only temporary capture at an initial distance equal to about twice the present value. However, if such a capture took place sufficiently early in the development of the solar system, there would still have remained in the neighbourhood of the orbit of the Earth a proportion of the original disc-material not collected into planets together with small aggregations of it. Capture of only a little of this by the Earth, and particularly by the Moon, now orbiting about the Earth, would have the effect of drawing them together because of the negligible angular momentum brought in, and render them permanently bound by their mutual gravitation against the disruptive tendency of solar action. Otherwise, under purely conservative dynamical forces, which are all that would remain operative after several aeons of existence of the solar system, a captured moon must eventually escape again and return to its status as an independent planet.

A mechanism of perhaps more speculative kind that might well occur and could completely overcome the difficulty would result from the fact that from time to time the solar system, in its path round the galaxy, must have passed through innumerable cosmical gas-and-dust clouds, when a vast hydrogen-atmosphere could come temporarily to surround the Sun and extend to planetary distances. Within such a cloud, the Earth itself would form a local concentration giving an extended atmosphere to it of radial dimensions comparable with its gravitational range of action in competition with the Sun. This distance is of order $(M/3m')^{1/3}c'$, which remarkably enough is equal to almost four times the present lunar distance. Such an atmosphere would produce a drag on the motion of the Moon through it, and thereby draw the Moon in towards the Earth, just as the orbit of an artificial satellite moving in the present high terrestrial atmosphere is gradually rounded up and reduced in dimensions, and the body eventually brought back to Earth. This possibility poses a problem difficult of rigorous analysis, but it is undoubted that dissipation of the energy of the Moon would occur in such an extensive atmosphere with the effect of drawing the satellite in, and then during the lengthier periods of time when the density of interplanetary gas had reverted to an almost negligible value where planetary motions are concerned, as at present, tidal friction would dominate to drive the Moon outwards again.

The present rate of dissipation of energy through lunar tidal action follows at once from (20) since it is the work done by the couple $-N$ acting upon the Earth and this is simply $-N(\omega - n)$, which is equal to about 3.3×10^{19} erg/sec. The energy so lost, which will be converted into heat, is of course extracted from the rotatory energy of the Earth.

Returning now to the solution of (18) and (19) for the term $N' + \omega\dot{C}$, it is readily found that

$$N'(\text{total}) + \omega\dot{C} = (-0.52 \pm 0.44) \times 10^{23}\,\text{cgs}. \quad \ldots(27)$$

This result brings to full exposure a remarkable but hitherto unrevealed consequence of the equations for ν and ν' as presented in all previous discussions. If, as has always been assumed, C is constant, then it is seen that N' turns out to be negative. On the earlier values, mainly from the work of Fotheringham, relied upon by de Sitter and Jeffreys, which were

$$\nu = (10''.44 \pm 0''90)\mathrm{cy}^{-2} , \quad \nu' = (3''.60 \pm 0''.48)\mathrm{cy}^{-2}$$

solution of the equations corresponding to (15) and (16) would yield

$$N'(\text{total}) + \omega\dot{C} = (-1.40 \pm 0.46) \times 10^{23} \text{ cgs}, \quad \ldots(28)$$

and with C constant, as tacitly assumed, N' would have taken a still more strongly unacceptable negative value had it ever been explicitly solved for, a simple step inexplicably not made during some fifty years discussion of the theory.

It is clearly important to consider how the two elements of $N' + \omega\dot{C}$ can be separated, which needs introduction of further considerations. The solar couple has been written N'(total) because it is known to be the sum of two quite different contributions : the tidal friction part, depending on the solid and liquid elements of the Earth already discussed, which acts to <u>decelerate</u> the rotation of the Earth, and a thermal-pressure part caused by solar heating that produces a non-negligible tide in the terrestrial atmosphere. The existence of such an additional tide was first recognised by Kelvin in 1882, and surprisingly the phase of its maximum amplitude is such that the resulting couple, transmitted by friction to the body of the Earth, is <u>accelerative</u> acting to speed up the angular velocity. There is of course no corresponding lunar thermal couple. The amount of this solar couple has been calculated by a number of authors since the time of Kelvin, each arriving at slightly different numerical coefficients in the harmonic expression for the distribution of excess pressure over the surface of the Earth determined from meteorological measures. Here the value arrived at by Holmberg (1952) will be adopted, namely

$$N'(\text{thermal}) = -\,0.37 \times 10^{23} \text{ cgs}. \qquad \ldots.(29)$$

Holmberg attached no error-range to the result, but as the value itself is numerically smaller than the error-range in (27), any error in (29) will be unimportant. Clearly N'(thermal) is far too weak a couple to be able to render the tidal part of N' in (27) or (28) with $\dot{C} = 0$, sufficiently large to accord with either the equilibrium tide or the quadratic-friction value of N/N'. Using (29) to remove this part of the couple from N'(total) in (27) leaves

$$N'(\text{tidal}) + \omega\dot{C} = (-0.15 \pm 0.44) \times 10^{23} \text{ cgs} \quad \ldots.(30)$$

Now as has been seen, N' can be calculated from N by dimensional scaling if equilibrium tidal theory is used, which gives a factor $(4.774)^{-1}$, so that from (20)

$$N'(\text{tidal}) = (1.00 \pm 0.08) \times 10^{23} \text{ cgs.}$$

Relation (30) would then imply

$$\omega\dot{C} = (-1.15 \pm 0.47) \times 10^{23} \text{ cgs.} \quad \ldots.(31)$$

For quadratic friction, the theoretical ratio of N/N' is about 3.8, as earlier noted, and for this N'(tidal) = $(1.25 \pm 0.10) \times 10^{23}$ cgs. On this basis, therefore

$$\omega\dot{C} = (-1.40 \pm 0.47) \times 10^{23} \text{ cgs.} \quad \ldots.(32)$$

Thus whether the friction is linear or quadratic, $\omega\dot{C}$ is strongly negative to an extent far larger than could be attributed to the effect of errors of observation. The fictitious couple $-\omega\dot{C}$ is more than thrice the magnitude of the Kelvin thermal couple, and for either type of friction is greater than the corresponding solar tidal couple N'.

This highly important term in $\dot{C}$ has been omitted by error from the theory as presented by previous authors, and clearly in view of its magnitude the oversight entirely vitiates their discussions and conclusions. On the ancient-eclipse data, it is seen to be inescapable that $\omega\dot{C}$ is strongly negative, and the moment-of-inertia of the Earth therefore decreasing at such a rate as to bring about effects comparable with those produced by tidal friction. The numerical value of the various terms involved (omitting error-ranges) in order of decreasing magnitude, and thus in order of relative importance in the theory, are as follows :

N (lunar tidal couple $= 4.74 \times 10^{23}$ cgs

$-\omega\dot{C}$ (quadratic friction) $= 1.40 \times 10^{23}$ cgs

N'(quadratic friction) $= 1.25 \times 10^{23}$ cgs

$-\omega\dot{C}$ (linear friction) $= 1.15 \times 10^{23}$ cgs

N'(linear friction) $= 1.00 \times 10^{23}$ cgs

N'(thermal atmospheric tide) $= 0.37 \times 10^{23}$ cgs

It is seen that, on either basis of tidal friction, the fictitious couple $-\omega\dot{C}$ is second in importance only to N itself.

In their discussions of the observational material, a number of authors have exhibited the results in terms of the several individual contributions to the total rate of change of the angular velocity of the Earth, $\dot{\omega}$. To show the present results in this form, the value of $\dot{\omega}$ (total) can be obtained at once from equation (1) for ν', since as earlier seen n' is negligible. This yields

$$\dot{\omega}(\text{total}) = -5.24 \times 10^{-22} \text{ (radian) } s^{-2}. \qquad \text{.... (34)}$$

Now $\dot{\omega}$(total) will be the sum of three components: namely the acceleration caused by the lunar couple $-N$, which may be denoted by $\dot{\omega}_m$; that produced by the total solar couple, $\dot{\omega}_s$; and the intrinsic component $\dot{\omega}_i$ which arises from the decreasing moment-of-inertia. With the present $C = 8.04 \times 10^{44}$ cgs, the values of (33) lead at once to the following sets of values for the two types of tidal friction, and also is shown the proportionate rate of intrinsic acceleration $\dot{\omega}_i/\omega$, which it is usual to express in the unit 10^{-11} per year.

Equilibrium Tidal Theory	Quadratic Tidal Friction
$\dot{\omega}_m = -5.90 \times 10^{-22}\ s^{-2}$	$\dot{\omega}_m = -5.90 \times 10^{-22}\ s^{-2}$
$\dot{\omega}_s = -0.78 \times 10^{-22}\ s^{-2}$	$\dot{\omega}_s = -1.09 \times 10^{-22}\ s^{-2}$
$\dot{\omega}_i = +1.44 \times 10^{-22}\ s^{-2}$	$\dot{\omega}_i = +1.75 \times 10^{-22}\ s^{-2}$
$\dot{\omega}_{i/\omega} = 6.23 \times 10^{-11}\ yr^{-1}$	$\dot{\omega}_{i/\omega} = 7.57 \times 10^{-11}\ yr^{-1}$

Demonstration from the observations of the existence of this essentially positive <u>intrinsic</u> component of acceleration in the rotation of the Earth seems to have been first achieved by Dicke (1966), about a year after its prediction by the present author by means of entirely different theoretical considerations of planetary structure and evolution (1965). With equilibrium tidal theory, Dicke arrived effectively at the value $\dot{\omega}_{i/\omega} = 5.8 \times 10^{-11}$ per year after adjustment here for a slightly incorrect value adopted for N/N'. Similarly for quadratic friction, Dicke found 6.7×10^{-11} per year using here the value 3.8 later calculated (1968) by R.R. Newton in this case. On the supposition of Dicke that one-third of the tidal friction occurs in open oceans and deep seas (linear friction) and two-thirds in shallow seas (quadratic friction), this would have led to 6.4×10^{-11} per year, while the two values herein arrived at similarly combined give 7.0×10^{-11} per year. The small differences between these various values are unimportant in view of the errors inevitably associated with the original observations.

So the results as a whole lead to the definitive conclusion that a term $\dot{\omega}_i$ of substantial magnitude is forming part of the total value of $\dot{\omega}$, and hence that the moment-of-inertia of the Earth is undergoing corresponding decrease. The numerical rate of this decrease follows at once from (10), which gives $\dot{C} = -C\dot{\omega}_{i/\omega}$: hence for the two types of friction

$$\begin{cases} \dot{C} = -\,1.54 \times 10^{27}\ \text{cgs (equilibrium tidal theory)}, \\ \dot{C} = -\,1.88 \times 10^{27}\ \text{cgs (quadratic friction)}. \end{cases} \quad \ldots (36)$$

Thus the conclusion from ancient-eclipse data combined with tidal theory, on either the linear or quadratic basis in the latter case, is that the moment-of-inertia of the Earth is diminishing at a rate somewhere between 1.5×10^{27} cgs and 1.9×10^{27} cgs. The problem of what is causing this decrease manifestly lies outside the province of tidal-friction theory, and can be tackled only by considerations of the internal physical structure and evolution of the Earth which will be the subject of the following Chapter.

REFERENCES AND NOTES

Calame O. & Mulholland J.D. Science 199, 977, 1978.

Holmberg E.R.R. Mon.Not.Roy.Astron.Soc. Geophys.Suppl. 6, 325, 1952.

Dicke R.H. The Earth-Moon System, 160, NASA Publ., Plenum Press, New York, 1966.

Flandern T.C.van, Mon.Not.Roy.Astron.Soc.170, 333, 1975.

Fotheringham J.K. Mon.Not.Roy.Astron.Soc.80, 578, 1920, and 81, 104, 1921.

Jeffreys H. The Earth, edns 1-6, Cambridge, 1924-1976.

It may be emphasised that the use of the equation

$$\frac{d}{dt}(C\omega) = -N - N'$$

is in no way a special assumption. The form

$$C\frac{d\omega}{dt} = -N - N'$$

is simply a mistake of dynamics making the tacit assumption that C is constant. Strange to relate, the error seems to have escaped notice for over fifty years. Ironically enough, had the correct analysis been made at the outset, it would have revealed a diminishing moment-of-inertia and thereby have lent seeming support to the thermal-contraction theory for mountains, invalid though that theory is for other reasons.

Kelvin W. Proc. Roy. Soc. Edinburgh 11, 396, 1882.

Lyttleton R.A. The Effect on the Lunar Orbit of Meteoritic Accretion, Icarus 1, 137, 1962.

Lyttleton R.A. On the Phase-Change Hypothesis of the Structure of the Earth, Proc.Roy.Soc.A287, 471,1965.
See especially Section 8, p.486.

Lyttleton R.A. & Fitch J.P. On the Accelerations of the Moon and Sun, and the Origin of Mountains, The Moon & Planets, 18, 223, 1978.

Lyttleton R.A. Relation of a Contracting Earth to the Accelerations of the Sun and Moon, The Moon & Planets, 16, 41, 1976.

Morrison L.V. & Ward C.G. Mon.Not.Roy.Astron.Soc. 173, 183, 1975.

Muller P.M. Determination of Tidal Accelerations of the Earth and Moon, NASA,Lunar Program Office,1976.
This paper gives comprehensive references to all aspects of the problem.

Newton R.R. Geophys.Journ.Roy.Astron.Soc.14, 527, 1968.

Oesterwinter C.A. & Cohen C.J. Celest.Mech.5, 317,1972.

Stephenson F.R. & Muller P.M. Accelerations of the Sun and Moon from Early Astronomical Observations, p.459 et seq. in History of the Earth's Rotation, Wiley & Sons, 1975.

Stephenson F.R. Pre-Telescopic Astronomical Observations, p.5 et seq. in Tidal Friction and the Earth's Rotation, Springer-Verlag, 1978.
Dr Stephenson informs the writer that the values of ν and ν' include some allowance for records of transits of Mercury which improves their accuracy still further.
Although Stephenson and Muller reject almost all the ancient eclipses accepted by Fotheringham, and relied upon by de Sitter and Jeffreys, it is remarkable enough that these early values, of ν = (10".44 ± 0".90) per century^2 and ν' = (3.60 ± 0".48) per century^2, are not all that much different from the modern values based on far more refined data. If the arithmetic is re-worked with these early values, the conclusion that C is negative emerges rather more strongly.

Williams J.G., Sinclair W.S., & Yoder C.F. Geophys.Res. Letters 5(11), 943, 1978.

5

The Phase-Change Hypothesis

The belief appears to have become more and more widely held that the liquid core of the Earth is mainly composed of iron, and therefore essentially different chemically from the solid mantle and outer shell. Its mass amounts to 31.4 per cent of the entire mass of the Earth. The iron-core hypothesis seems to have developed in a general way following experimental measures of the constant of gravitation G since the eighteenth century. As the acceleration of gravity g at the surface of the Earth is readily measurable and is related to G by $g = GM/r_S^2$, then if the value of G becomes otherwise available this leads to the value of M and hence to the overall mean-density of the Earth, now known to be 5.52 g/cm^3. In passing, it may be of some historic interest to note that Newton himself estimated that the mean-density was between 5 and 6 g/cm^3 from considerations of the relative masses of the planets (Principia, Book iii, Propsns VIII & X), but he did not attempt to suggest iron as the main constituent. As the known densities of surface-rocks average only about 2.7 g/cm^3, and since iron had already somehow come to be thought specially abundant, it was assumed that the Earth must contain a high proportion of iron and possibly some nickel too, though conjecture as to the location within the Earth could scarcely be attempted at that stage. The presence of a terrestrial magnetic field also seemed to lend support to the idea in view of the phenomenon of ferromagnetism.

Because of the known large temperature-gradient in the surface-layers, which could be directly measured in mines, but in the complete absence of any knowledge of radioactivity, it was inferred at one time that the whole Earth at depths greater than about 50 km must be in mixed molten and gaseous forms in order to give the observed outflow of heat. No more than about 1 per cent of the entire mass would accordingly have been in solid form with strength to provide this shallow crust at the exterior, and on this basis it seemed readily understandable that heavy elements, such as free iron and nickel, would be able to sink to the centre to give hydrostatic equilibrium. But it was not long before the study of earthquake-waves was to dispose completely of this primitive picture, for not only did wave-theory reveal that most of the Earth was more rigid than steel, but that by far the greater outer part of it, the mantle and outer-shell, transmitted both primary and secondary elastic waves, the so-called P- and S- waves, the latter of which can be propagated only in a solid. The next important discovery was made in 1906 by Oldham, and since confirmed in detail by all subsequent work, that there exists a large core in which no S-waves are transmitted, and hence that it is liquid in form. It seems then to have gradually come to be believed that it was in this liquid core that the desired iron must be located, though it is extremely difficult to trace in the literature the growth and development of the idea which seems to have come about rather through oral geophysical lore or credo than from considerations reasoned in scientific terms. Thus in the first edition of <u>The Earth</u> (1924), there appears to be no mention of the core at all (certainly it is not referenced), nor to its discovery in 1906. A few references to Oldham himself occur, but none to this particular work by him, and needless to add no statement of any suggested compositional nature. Five years later, in the Encyclopaedia Britannica (14th Edn, 1929), in discussing the mean-density of the Earth, Jeffreys writes that the high value "indicates an interior composed of heavy metals, especially iron, since this is the commonest heavy metal in the crust", and although the existence of a liquid core is later mentioned, its composition is not suggested to be iron or anything specific. Short of direct extraction of a sample from the core, a feat not yet in sight of accomplishment, no means of chemical identification of its material has become available, for seismic data can yield only the elastic properties, not the precise composition. Yet some claim that the evidence now favouring a metallic iron core is quite overwhelming, though curiously enough they omit to supply any indication of the nature of this overwhelming evidence.

Such arguments as have been advanced, however, are found to have little force when examined with other than the eye of faith. For example, iron itself, as aforesaid, was considered to be an abundant terrestrial constituent, and thus the most probable candidate, but it becomes far less abundant if the core is not actually iron, and the argument is seen to have been in some degree circular. Moreover, the abundance of the elements cosmically suggests no more than a few per cent of iron amongst all the various heavy elements, while allowance for Fe in combination with other elements in terrestrial rocks would bring the proportion up nearer to forty per cent if the core were iron, and present the Earth as a strange body indeed amongst cosmic objects. Strong support was also thought to be supplied by the composition of meteorites, despite their origin being one of the most inscrutable problems in the solar system. Meteorites can be classified roughly as either <u>stones</u> or <u>irons</u>, but of meteorites <u>actually seen to fall</u>, which selection can alone provide reliable indications of the true proportions of each variety, since iron meteorites are far more easily recognisable on subsequent discovery than are stony ones, less than 3 per cent are irons. Iron meteorites, however, constitute by far the majority of museum-specimens, for the same simple reason, and this has tended to give the false impression of their actually being more abundant. In view of the proportion of the terrestrial mass in the core, the meteorite-argument would if anything tell strongly against the core being iron, even if it were otherwise acceptable to suppose that the Earth were built up from such bodies. As regards meteorites falling in recent times, which presumably has been occurring with at least equal frequency in the remote past, the last place from which they could be extracted would seem to be the core of some hypothetical planet similar to the Earth, wherein they would be buried under about 3,000 km of solid rock.

The tempting hypothesis that the magnetic field of the Earth results from ferromagnetism was disposed of when the existence was established of the so-called Curie-point temperature of iron and nickel-iron alloys, at which temperatures magnetism is destroyed, and that the effect of pressure on these critical temperatures is much too small to allow permanent magnetism to persist within the Earth. Over and above these considerations, the magnetic field is known to undergo comparatively rapid changes and motions, such as the westward drift, which would seem could not possibly occur if its source were rigidly connected to the solid body of the Earth. Some dynamo-mechanism within the liquid core, possibly driven by precession, at present seems the most likely explanation.

Such mechanism, if relying on currents in liquid iron, obviously would be at least equally effective if the nature of the core-material were a phase-change to a metallic liquid form of the mantle-material. This in essence is the Ramsey proposal, and it would provide an entirely acceptable basis for any process of generation of the field by electrical currents in the terrestrial core. The tendency noted here to assume an excessive abundance of iron has hampered other related areas : for example, Eddington in his initial attempts on the theory of stellar structure adopted the molecular weight of iron for that of stellar material, and it enters to the fourth power in the expression for the luminosity. When the importance of ionisation was realised, precise identification seemed less relevant, but the modified supposition that the iron would be nearly fully ionised still suggested a mean molecular-weight of about 2, and delayed recognition of the extent to which hydrogen was really the principal constituent with heavy elements rare by comparison.

The Moon, as already seen to have most probably been captured early on from an orbit close to that of the Earth, has a mean-density of only 3·34 g/cm^3, and therefore cannot contain a percentage of iron in the least comparable with that claimed to be in the terrestrial core (31 per cent), for if it did, not only would the mean-density be much higher, but the lunar radius would be nearly 300 kilometres less than the observed value. For Mars with a mean-density of only 3·95 g/cm^3 (despite its being about 9 times the mass of the Moon) a similar conclusion holds, for if Mars were 31 per cent iron the radius would be about 150 km less than the actual value. But perhaps the most fatal blow against the core being of iron is that the seismic data show that, whatever the chemical composition may be, the uncompressed density of its material, as has been seen, is only slightly greater than 6 g/cm^3, whereas iron and nickel, even in liquid form have density 15% and 30% greater than this, respectively. Attempts have also been made in recent years to identify the core-material as iron by data from shock-wave experiments, but the physical arguments relied upon are thermodynamically quite unsound. In the seismic case, infinitesimal waves and pressure-differences are propagated through material already under high pressure, and in the core at high temperature, whereas in experiments with shock-waves a severe shock moves into unstressed material at ordinary temperature. The treatment-history to be accorded to a volume-element of material is totally different in the two cases, and chemical identification based on a mere very rough comparison of velocities cannot be made. This is confirmed by the fact that if the method were accepted at its face value as valid, its arguments would lead even more strongly to the conclusion that the mantle is made of aluminium.

The foregoing discussion lists some of the doubts surrounding the iron-core hypothesis, over and above the general consideration that the chance is vanishingly small that the solution of a deep problem of nature would have been guessed correctly more or less at the very outset from the slenderest of clues, such as the high mean-density of the Earth, as the only guide. The widespread acceptance of the idea, which it has nevertheless achieved, is readily explicable, however, as a manifestation of the Gold-effect plus the standard servo-mechanisms brought to bear which augment this (Lyttleton 1979). The lack of success associated with the iron-core idea might be thought to have served to make any alternative hypothesis welcome, but in fact, although thirty years have gone by since Ramsey's proposal of the phase-change hypothesis, it has largely been ignored or too lightly dismissed, with the iron-core notion meanwhile tenaciously adhered to despite the obvious difficulties on all sides that ensue from it, and its complete lack of any predictive power.

To describe briefly the general nature of the phase change hypothesis as first advanced by Ramsey in 1948 to 1950, it may be noticed first that it is intuitively obvious that material cannot have infinite strength, and that if sufficient pressure is applied to a volume-element of matter then at some stage a breakdown of its atomic structure is to be expected. By discarding the outer-shell of electrons, the atomic-volume of a substance can be much reduced, and such a process would involve the loss of at least part of the molecular and crystal bindings. But if the applied pressure is high enough, the work done by it during compression can clearly more than compensate for the loss of binding-energy, and when equilibrium is next achieved the state of the substance will be a metal of considerably higher density. The transition from a molecular phase to a metallic phase under pressure is essentially different from temperature-ionisation as occurs in stellar gas, for example. Prior to Ramsey's work, theoretical studies of this pressure-transition had been made successfully only for hydrogen, and these had shown that when the pressure reaches 0.7×10^{12} dyn/cm^2, the density suddenly increases from about 0.4 g/cm^3 in the original state to about 0.8 g/cm^3 in the new state with the hydrogen now in a metallic phase, while other similar investigations found an increase by a rather larger factor. This increase in density by a considerable factor is specially to be emphasised, for where planetary structure is concerned, if a phase-change between one zone and a contiguous deeper zone occurs, a density-increase by a factor in excess of 1.5 is critical for the nature of the outcome of the change, as will be seen in detail later. In fact, an increase of density by such an amount occurs at present in the Earth across the mantle-core boundary, the density at the base of the solid mantle being 5.68 g/cm^3 and at the outermost layer of the liquid core 9.43 g/cm^3, an increase in the ratio 1.66. The explicit proposal of the phase-change hypothesis is that the core-material represents a metallic liquid phase of mantle-material, and therefore having chemically the same composition as the mantle, apart from the possible slight reservation of some hydrostatic differentiation next to be explained.

As earlier mentioned, within the liquid core is a small central core with a further discontinuity outside and at its surface. There is some evidence that this innermost core may even be solid. Its radius is about 1250 km, compared with 3473 km for the liquid core itself, while its mass is about 0.138×10^{27} g, compared with 1.876×10^{27}g, for the whole core, which means only about 7 per cent of the latter. On the phase change hypothesis, it could be that this inner core consists of the heaviest components that have settled out to produce hydrostatic equilibrium after having descended through the liquid core, in the manner assumed would have happened in an Earth originally in molten form.

It was shown by Ramsey on general physical grounds, which will be summarised later in this chapter, that for most substances the crucial pressures to effect the transition to a metallic phase are of the order of 10^{12} dyn/cm^2, much as first ionisation potentials for many elements are of the same order at a few volts. However, there are substances for which both metallic and non-metallic phases exist at atmospheric pressure, as for instance arsenic and tin. The familiar form of the latter is the metal, but if it is held at a temperature below about -18°C it eventually transforms into a non-metallic greyish powder, known to museum-curators as <u>tin-pest</u>. Reliably accurate theoretical calculations of the pressure at which complex substances, such as terrestrial rocks, would undergo the phase-change are beyond present capabilities. But recently there has emerged, from the work of Bell, Mao, and others at the Carnegie Geophysical Institution, the highly interesting possibility of reaching experimentally static pressures comparable with those prevailing in the core of the Earth, which range from 1.37×10^{12} dyn/cm^2 at the outer boundary up to about 3.6×10^{12} dyn/cm^2 at the centre. It is most important to realise that only results based on static pressures are likely to provide suitable indications, for geophysical purposes, of the behaviour of materials under high pressures. The physical effects of transient dynamical or impulsive high-pressures, such as accompany passage of a shockwave through material, are not only by their nature difficult to subject to direct measurement but are also difficult of interpretation in usable form. Thus a stone can be skimmed across a sheet of water, with surface contact-pressure impulses produced that can sustain it against gravity, but results for this phenomenon could scarcely be applicable even to initial effects if the stone were placed at rest on the surface of the water.

The static high-pressures referred to above are achieved by means of a diamond-anvil press, as the apparatus has been termed. So far actual experiments on sample-materials have been carried out it seems only up to about 0.5×10^{12} dyn/cm^2, but these have already shown that for some substances the molecular bonds are readily broken down. The consequences of the most easily reached high-pressures are first being studied with this instrument, naturally enough, but calibrations have shown that sustained static pressures as high as 1.7×10^{12} dyn/cm^2 are within the powers of the equipment, and simulated core-conditions seem to be definitely attainable in the near future. The apparatus is so constructed that the diamond-elements that compress the sample are transparent to injected laser-beams, and thus the temperatures may be adjusted as well as the applied pressure.

One of the most remarkable features of the mantle-core interface is its extreme sharpness, the transition occurring in vanishingly small depth, and this is difficult if not impossible to reconcile merely with a change in composition, though it is readily understandable within the phase-change theory, as Ramsey demonstrated. The reflecting powers of this boundary for seismic waves exhibit wellnigh mirrorlike perfection, and as Jeffreys first showed (1945) this is not at all what would be expected if the density merely increased more or less continuously over a modest depth, as it would if a change of composition were involved. Ramsey later showed that if a change with depth to an entirely different substance (rock to iron) occurred, then at the temperature prevailing in the core, which could approach 10,000 K, the density-change would not be sharp at all, but take place gradually through a depth of some 300 km, and there would result diffraction and dispersion-effects quite inconsistent with the known properties of seismic waves at and near this interface. Ramsey also pointed out that if by any means it were possible to achieve so complete and sharp a chemical separation as the seismic data would demand, as for instance the original idea of hydrostatic separation in an all-molten Earth, then the elements of the core-material should be very rare if not completely absent elsewhere, which of course is known not to be the case for iron at or near the surface. It may also be noted that the present liquid core could not represent the yet unsolidified portion of an all-molten Earth, for conduction of heat proceeds so slowly that cooling and solidification from the surface to this depth would require a time far longer than the currently accepted age of the Earth, while some analyses of the cooling of a hypothetically initially molten Earth claim that solidification would start at the centre. Either result would obviously render the hypothesis of a liquid-iron core difficult of acceptance. On the phase-change hypothesis, it is rising temperature through radioactive energy-release, augmented by the accompanying release of gravitational energy through contraction of the planet, which operating under the high-pressure conditions are the agencies responsible for bringing about the liquid metallic nature of the core. Since the radioactive elements concerned possess half-lives comparable with the age of the Earth, the processes are still active, with the core continuing to grow but the Earth as a whole contracting.

Yet another notable success of the phase-change theory is its ability to account for well-established but hitherto inexplicably curious anomalies in the velocities of both P-waves and S-waves in the mantle near the core-boundary. Both speeds fail to go on increasing at the expected rate as the interface is approached, while strangely enough no similar anomaly is found to occur in the velocity of the P-waves immediately inside the boundary. There exist no S-waves, of course. Fig. 4 illustrates the phenomena. The phase-change theory, as Ramsey proved, readily explains these seeming anomalies by showing that immediately outside the boundary of the core the value of the bulk-modulus will be reduced below its otherwise expected value by about 1%, and the discrepancy diminish exponentially with height above the interface, partly because the temperature may decrease somewhat outwards, but mainly because the excitation-energy increases. The rigidity will suffer a similar change of comparable amount and give rise to the seeming anomaly in the S-waves. Moreover these anomalies occur only on the lower-pressure side of the transition, for the reason that on the high-pressure side the excitation-energy is necessarily always very much higher as a result of the large decrease in volume that is characteristic of the phase-change to metallic form. These seemingly strange properties of the seismic wave-speeds were already well known but had long remained without satisfactory explanation, and it was a major triumph that Ramsey's theory provided a physical reason for them. A further velocity-anomaly, and one even more marked, occurs through about 100 km in depth immediately outside the small innermost core, where the pressure exceeds 3×10^{12} dyn/cm^2. In view of the difference in behaviour of the P-wave velocity, as compared with outside the core-mantle interface (Fig. 4), it would not seem safe to rule out the possibility that this may in part result from differentiation by composition with changing admixture over this

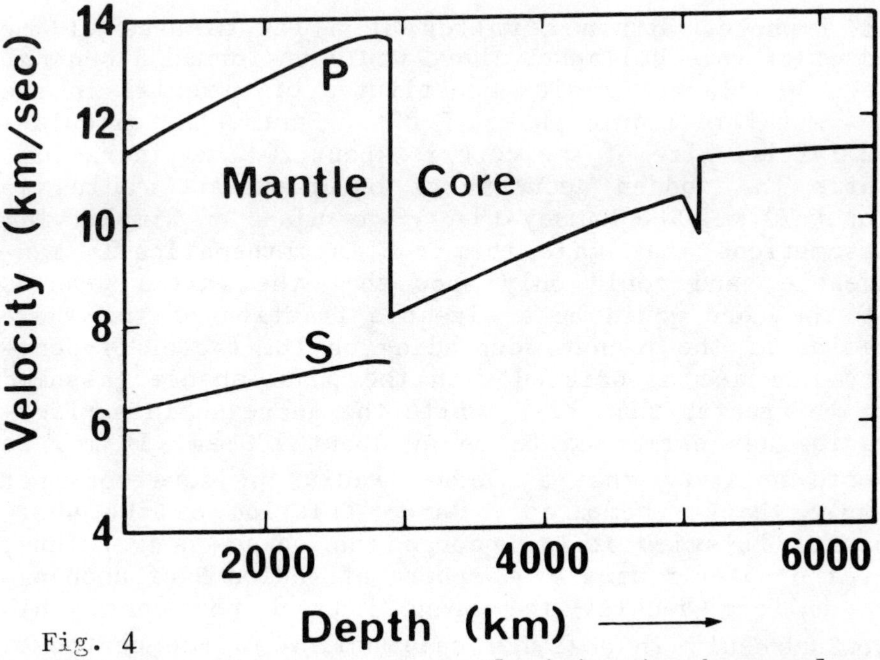

Fig. 4
Behaviour of seismic wave-velocities in the mantle.

depth of some 100 km. Ramsey himself favoured a second phase-change under the greater pressure as the explanation, but within a liquid core it is certain that the substances of greatest density would automatically fall to the most central region. This innermost core is claimed to be solid, but as waves in it can be excited only by great earthquakes able to vibrate the whole Earth, the data are limited and difficult of secure interpretation.

When it comes to applying the phase-change hypothesis to the mechanical equilibrium and internal mass-distribution of the Earth (and other terrestrial planets Chap. 6), further convincing evidence in its favour emerges. In the first place, Ramsey established the remarkable result that, if the increase of density associated with the change of phase is by a factor exceeding 1.5, then there would occur with gradually increasing mass of the planet, or gradually increasing internal temperature with constant mass, a sudden catastrophic collapse to smaller size affecting the planet as a whole. Within a matter of a few minutes of the onset of this collapse, there would be formed a central core of 'large' radius constituted of material in the new metallic liquid phase. For the Earth, the calculated initial size of the core is about 2040 km in radius, while the sudden decrease of outer-surface radius is about 70 km. The Ramsey-theory was based on simplifying assumptions that made the problem mathematically manageable, and could only show that the initial radius of the core would be a sizeable fraction of the whole radius of the planet, depending on the factor of density-increase associated with the phase-change (assumed to be greater than 1.5), while the decrease in surface-radius was estimated to be by about 100 km. It may be worth noticing that a 'large' radius of core does not imply that a comparably large fraction of the whole mass will immediately undergo the phase-change. Thus, if the outer radius of a sphere of radius R of unchanged uniform density is expanded by 1 per cent, this would result in a (spherical) hollow in the centre of radius 0.31R, and reversely, if the outer radius were decreased by 1 per cent, this could be accommodated by doubling the density in a central sphere of radius 0.31R, though only 3 per cent of the mass would be superimposed there.

The theory leading to Ramsey's conclusions and the nature of the equilibrium-configurations and stabilities involved can be illustrated by consideration of a bead under gravity sliding on a wire in the form of a quartic curve lying in a vertical plane (Fig. 5). The points where the bead can rest in equilibrium will be determinable by means of the roots of the derived cubic equation, and if the equation for the quartic contains some slowly changing parameter then at first the cubic could have only one real root, and there would be just a single place at which the bead could rest. Next, for a range of the parameter, the cubic could come to have three real roots, and then later still with further change of the parameter it could revert to possessing one real root, as illustrated in the diagram. Thus to begin with on curve 11 there will be just the one position A for the bead, and clearly a stable position

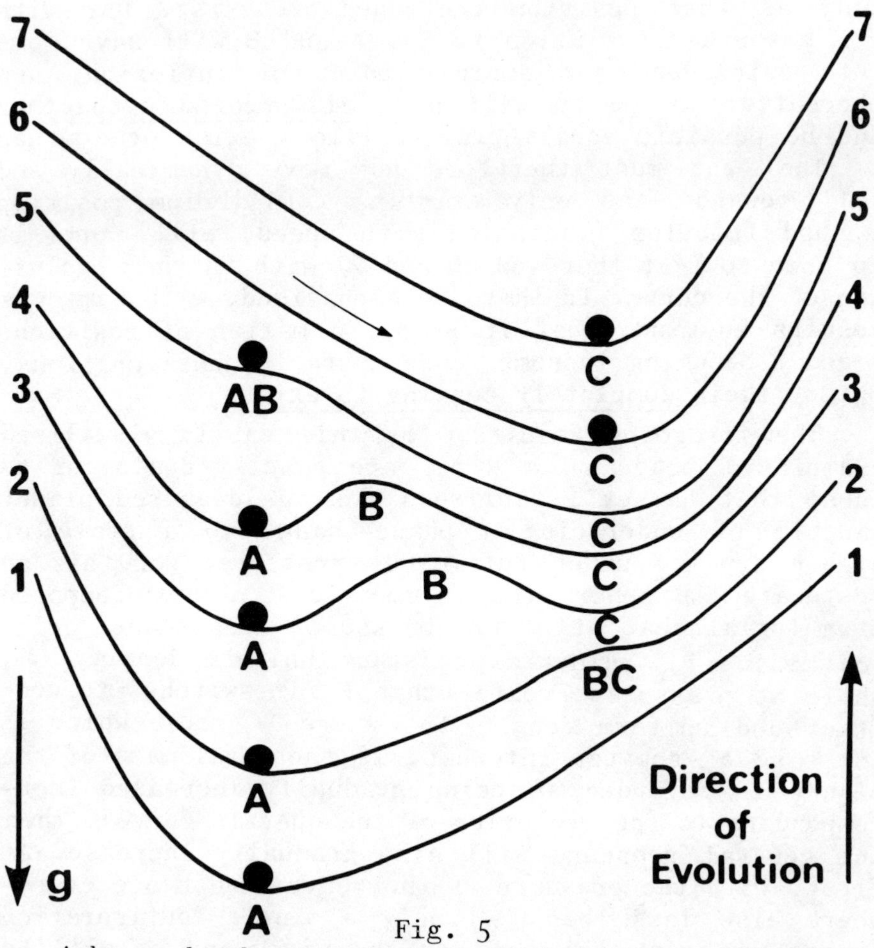

Fig. 5
A heavy bead on a slowly-evolving quartic curve.

for the form of curve adopted. As the curve evolves to the shape 22, an inflexion BC now appears corresponding to two new but coincident equilibrium positions, B and C. These would proceed with further evolution to separate into two possible equilibrium-positions, shown at B and C on curves 33 and 44, in addition to the original A. Clearly position-B is unstable while C is stable, but although the bead could rest at either of these points if placed there, if left to itself it would continue to remain at the original minimum A so long as that position continued to exist. But with still further evolution to 55, A and B will have come into coincidence at another point of inflexion, and thereafter as on 66 will have disappeared altogether and no possible equilibrium-positions exist other than C. The bead must therefore now move dynamically and fall towards the only existing equilibrium position C, and friction (vanishing with speed) will cause it to come to rest there on 66 and 77 with further evolution of the curve. It is to be emphasised, with Ramsey's results in mind, that it is not a matter of positions A and B becoming in some sense unstable configurations, but of their completely ceasing to exist.

The foregoing results, for this easily visualised example of beads on a wire, are exactly analogous to those that Ramsey established for an idealised planet capable of undergoing a phase-change to a state of higher density under sufficient pressure. For this he postulated a spherically symmetrical planet composed of material that at static pressures less than a critical value P_c maintains constant uniform density ρ, while at pressures greater than P_c it switches to constant and uniform density $\lambda\rho$, where $\lambda > 1.5$, which is the case of greater interest. If the total mass of the planet is regarded as being gradually increased (corresponding to the evolution of the quartic curve), then the central pressure will also gradually increase. At first, with the pressure at the centre and hence everywhere else less than P_c, only a single configuration exists, as with the bead on the wire, and it will be a 1-zone planet of density ρ. But when the slowly increasing mass m passes beyond a certain critical value, $m = M_1$ say, the Ramsey-theory showed that three possible configurations come to exist. One of these has central pressure less than P_c and thus is single-zoned of density ρ, while the other two have central pressures greater than P_c, and therefore are two-zoned with cores of density $\lambda\rho$. In Fig.6 these are denoted by A, B, and C, and exactly as for the bead, since A is initially stable, it follows that when all three configurations exist A and C are stable, while B is unstable. Although the planet could conceptually be placed in form B or

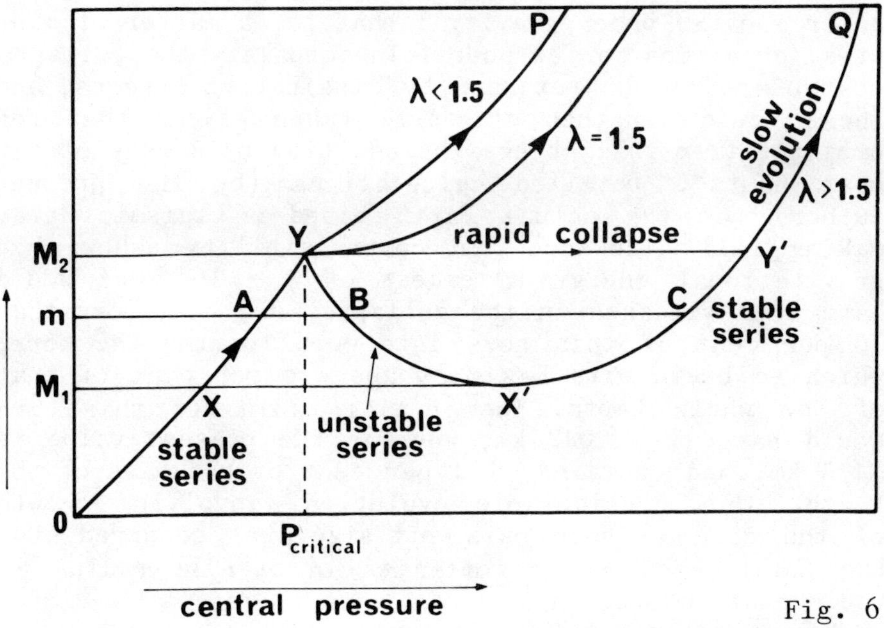

Fig. 6

The series of forms associated with the phase-change.

form C and be in equilibrium, it would in fact evolve along the series OA, and continue to do so, with further increase of mass until A and B merge into coincidence at Y for a certain critical value $m = M_2$ of the mass Then upon the slightest addition of mass, these two configurations cease to exist at all, and there remains state C as the only possible form of equilibrium available. Just as with the bead, the planet must move dynamically to this position by collapsing from its prior state of uniform density ρ, and in so doing develop what Ramsey termed a 'large core' of density $\lambda\rho$ having radius a sizeable fraction of the overall radius of the planet. The associated linear series of equilibrium configurations are shown schematically in Fig. 6 in which the total mass m as ordinate is plotted against the increasing central pressure. The time taken for the planet, if comparable with the Earth, to reach configuration Y' from Y, after A and B have ceased to exist will be, as Ramsey made clear, of the same order as the time taken for a free particle at the surface to fall through 100 km (the order of the decrease in outer radius) under gravity : that is, a matter of minutes, or at most a few hours. In actuality the collapse must of course be retarded by dissipative effects, and these would lengthen the time taken beyond that for a simple free fall; hence the addition by Ramsey of "at most hours". Detailed calculations (by the present author) for the actual Earth based on seismic data, making full allowance for compressibility, show that gravitational energy in excess of 5×10^{37} erg would have been released in the collapse, and that more than 70 per cent of this goes into work forming the core, which to begin with has mass about 6 per cent of that of the whole Earth. The initial radius of this core would have been 2042 km, whereas the present value is 3473 km, and contains 31.4 per cent of the mass of the Earth. Thus considerable evolution, involving growth of the core in both mass and size, has occurred. But the Earth as a whole <u>contracts</u> in overall radius as the evolution proceeds.

From seismic data, it can be shown that at the centre of the Earth just before collapse began $\lambda = 1.75$, thereby lending strong support to the Ramsey-theory. Across the mantle-core boundary, the density-jump at present is by a factor 1.66, and the representative-point for times subsequent to the collapse lies on the curve Y'Q in the diagram, with the Earth now thoroughly stable mechanically at every stage. Were $\lambda < 1.5$, no such collapse would occur. For the first phase-change in the Earth, associated with the 20°-discontinuity at 413 kilometre depth, and where the pressure is only 0.14×10^{12} dyn/cm^2, the value of λ is slightly greater than 1.07. For a small planet such as Mars, the central pressure is less than 0.3×10^{12} dyn/cm^2. In the course of the early growth stage, with the mass increasing rapidly by accretion from the dust-disc, the representative point in Fig.6 would move along the curve OY and then along YP. The point Y would be reached when the mass had become such that the central pressure was equal to P_C, and thereafter, since $\lambda < 1.5$ for this phase-change, the point would proceed rapidly along YP until increase of the mass had effectively stopped. All this would occur before any important radioactive heating had time to take place. There would be no sudden collapse, and both the mass and radius of the inner zone would increase continuously from zero. But with rising internal temperature from radioactive heating, the representative point would continue to move along YP, but now far more slowly. Since production of this 20°-discontinuity phase-change requires higher pressure with higher temperature, P_c itself would increase gradually, and the level of discontinuity within Mars would occur at greater depth. More of its material would revert to the less-dense phase, and the planet would gradually expand, as will be seen later (Chap. 8). Under evolution by increasing mass followed by internal heating at constant mass, only a single configuration and of stable form is possible at every stage, consisting of a single zone before the point Y is reached and of two zones thereafter.

As already noted, Ramsey adopted the assumption of two states for the material of densities ρ & $\lambda\rho$, and it is simple to demonstrate the existence of the critical value $\lambda = 1.5$. For let it be supposed that in a first state the planet is in hydrostatic equilibrium as a sphere of radius R and density ρ, and that a phase change occurs to a second state consisting of a small central region of radius R_1 and density $\lambda\rho$, with resulting new outer radius R_2. Then constancy of the total mass requires

$$R^3 = (\lambda - 1)R_1{}^3 + R_2{}^3. \qquad \ldots. \ (1)$$

From hydrostatic considerations, the pressure in the outer region $R_1 < r < R_2$ is given by

$$p(r) = \frac{4}{3}\pi G(\lambda - 1)\ \rho^2 R_1{}^3 (r^{-1} - R_2^{-1}) + \tfrac{2}{3}\pi G\rho^2 (R_2^2 - r^2). \qquad \ldots. \ (2)$$

Putting $R_1 = 0$ and $R_2 = R$, this will reduce to the expression for the pressure in the original state, and thus the central pressure p_o in that state is $2\pi G\rho^2 R^2/3$. Since $r = R_1$ is the interface-radius, it follows that the ratio of the interface-pressure p_{int} to the original central pressure is given by

$$\frac{p_{int}}{p_o} = 2(\lambda - 1)\left\{R_1^{\,2}R^{-2} - R_1^{\,3}R_2^{-1}R^{-2}\right\} + (R_2^{\,2} - R_1^{\,2})R^{-2} \ldots. \quad (3)$$

If now $R_1 = \theta R$, where θ is small (compared with unity), then making use of (1)

$$\frac{p_{int}}{p_o} = 1 + (2\lambda - 3)\theta^2 - \frac{8}{3}(\lambda - 1)\theta^3 + \ldots \qquad \ldots. \ (4)$$

Since the mass of the small central core is given by

$$m_c = {}^4/_3\pi\lambda\rho R^3\theta^3$$

it follows, omitting essentially positive factors, that

$$\frac{dp_{int}}{dm_c} \propto (\lambda - \frac{3}{2})\theta^{-1}, \qquad \ldots. \ (5)$$

and hence that, for m_c increasing from zero, p_{int} increases or decreases initially at infinite rate according as λ is greater or less than 1.5.

It will be shown later that for the Earth $\lambda = 1.75$, so that the pressure at the interface increases initially, and the rate being infinite, p_{int} will remain above p_o for a finite range of m_c. Thus sudden collapse to produce a core of finite size will occur : the representative point proceeding first along OY stably and steadily, then rapidly along YY' as the collapse occurs, and thereafter along Y'Q stably and steadily. On the other hand for a planet such as Mars it may be shown that $\lambda = 1.16$ at the centre, and no collapse would occur. Evolution would correspond first to OY until the critical pressure (or temperature) was reached at the centre, then core-formation in the new phase would commence and proceed continuously from zero, with evolution corresponding to the curve YP with only one configuration possible at any stage.

It was shown by Lighthill (1950) that the general situation remains unchanged if the material is compressible, with density increasing continuously with increasing pressure up to that required for the phase-change to occur, when the density then jumps by a factor λ. It was proved that if $\lambda < 1.5$, then again three states of equilibrium exist for a range of values of the total mass, and schematic representation of the series of possible configurations takes the same form as Fig. 6. This generalisation of the theory removed any doubt that might otherwise have been felt about the results derived by Ramsey as possibly being a product of the simplifying assumptions. The whole investigation provides a remarkable example of Poincaré's theory of linear series of configurations, and that planetary evolution can be represented in such elegant form might of itself suggest to some minds its probable correctness.

Ramsey further showed that the critical masses M_1 and M_2 (Fig. 6) depend on the internal temperature, and that evolution with increasing temperature, with the total mass remaining constant, will take the same schematic form as for increasing mass. Owing to radioactive energy-release throughout the interior, temperature would have been gradually rising since the Earth attained individuality as a planet, but so slow is transfer of heat by conduction that it is doubtful if more than a minute proportion of the energy released in the central regions has yet reached the surface to escape. As a result, these central regions of the Earth must be practically isothermal and possibly at a temperature of several thousand degrees, though any precise value is difficult of determination for the very reason that at the high pressures prevailing the density depends only on the pressure, as the seismic data can be shown to imply, any temperature-dependence remaining quite negligible in this regard, though definitely not in regard to conditions for the phase-change, which occurs at lowering pressure with rising temperature. Explanations may not be far to find. The proportionate density-change consequent on a temperature increase of a few thousand degrees is small compared with that produced by pressures of order 10^{12} dyn/cm^2. But on the other hand, if the core is isothermal, then an equation of state for its material will necessarily appear to involve only the pressure and density, while if in the mantle the temperature increases downwards, the resulting expansion-tendency could well be equivalent to a small negative pressure that could remain masked by the very high and increasing actual pressure.

The fact that λ is greater than 1.5 not only means that the Ramsey-collapse will occur, but also implies that the density of the liquid metallic phase ρ_L is considerably greater than ρ_S , the density of the solid phase represented by the mantle-material. On the other hand, at low pressures, for most materials, and certainly rocks and iron, ρ_S is greater than ρ_L , and thus the melting-point would be expected to increase with depth as the pressure increases. The rate of increase of the melting-point T_m, say, with pressure is determined by the thermodynamic equation

$$\frac{1}{T_m}\frac{dT_m}{dp} = \frac{1}{F}\left(\frac{1}{\rho_L} - \frac{1}{\rho_S}\right) \qquad \ldots\ldots (6)$$

where F is the latent heat of fusion for the transition from the solid to the liquid phase. Since $\rho_L < \rho_S$, it follows that proceeding downwards from the surface T_m will increase. It is established that the Earth is solid down to a depth of 2898 km, and if conditions continued downwards with only an ordinary liquid-phase possible, that is $\rho_L < \rho_S$, it is difficult to see why melting should occur anywhere, even if a change of composition to iron were involved, since for iron too $\rho_L < \rho_S$. However, on the phase-change hypothesis for the nature of the core, the metallic liquid phase is much denser than the solid phase, $\rho_L > \rho_S$ by the factor λ, the sign of the right-hand side of (1) is negative, and the melting point is lowered by increased pressure: that is, it would be least at the centre of the Earth. Thus even if for some hypothetical planet $1 < \lambda < 1.5$, so that there would be no sudden collapse but simply a transition to a liquid with $\rho_L > \rho_S$ melting would start at the centre when the temperature would have risen sufficiently through radioactive heating, with the melting-point now increasing outwards. The actual situation for the Earth would thus be illustrated in Fig. 7.

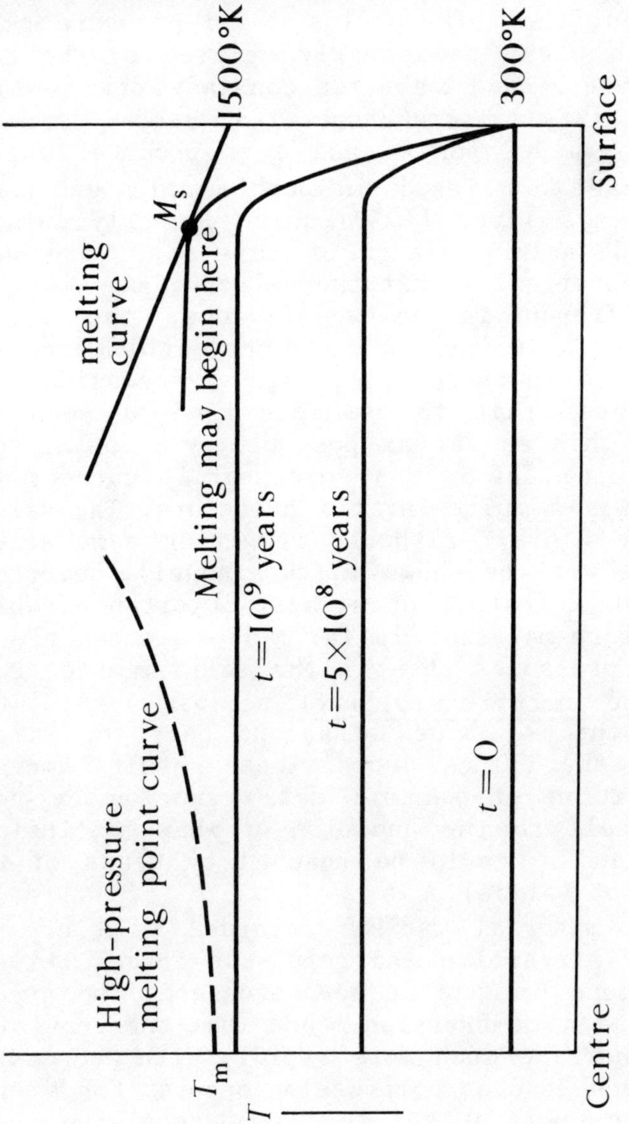

Fig. 7
Temperature changes within the Earth under radioactive heating.

It is not made clear in Ramsey's papers whether he intended identification of the initial 'large' core of configuration C with the present core, which would have precluded further evolution. Be that as it may, his next step was a theoretical investigation of compressibility applicable to terrestrial materials. It had already been suggested by Bullen that, except at discontinuities, the bulk-modulus k and pressure p inside the Earth might be linearly related by the form $k = k_0 + \alpha p$, where k_0 and α are two constants that could be adjusted to satisfy seismic properties. Bullen proposed some meaned-up values for k_0 and α to produce roughly the same linear form for k in both mantle and core. Ramsey some years later (1950) quite properly pointed out the unsatisfactory nature of this step, and went on to show theoretically that the values of k_0 must be essentially different in the two regions, the values found being 0.54×10^{12} dyn/cm^2 for the liquid core and 2.1×10^{12} dyn/cm^2 in the mantle. This very considerable difference showed that to use some kind of mean for k_0 and offset this as far as possible by adopting some best common value for α, not necessarily correct for either zone, was a quite-invalid procedure. The values of k_0 found by Ramsey, although requiring some slight adjustment (as will be shown in the sequel), nevertheless bring out a feature of highest importance, which is that the core-material is far more compressible at corresponding pressures than is the solid-mantle phase (k measures the incompressibility), because of the large difference in the two values of k_0 and only the slight difference in the values of α. These results emerged from consideration of seismic data, and Ramsey next addressed himself to the question of what conclusions concerning k and α could be reached by means of the atomic theory of solids.

Since the material can be regarded as a crystal for which the attractive and repulsive forces between neighbouring ions balance at zero-pressure, the strong capacity to resist compression means that the repulsive forces must increase much more rapidly with decreasing distance between ions as compression occurs. For a wide range of power-laws for the forces of repulsion, suggested by comparable materials of known properties, Ramsey was able to show that in both mantle and core α must take a value between 3 and 4, and he further established that, even if the core and mantle represented different materials, their values of α could not differ by much more than unity, while if they are different phases of the same material then the two values of α would differ by considerably less than unity and could even be practically equal. The discussion demonstrated theoretically that a relation of the form

$$k = k_o + \alpha p$$

would be expected to hold in the two zones, with almost equal values of α but importantly different values of k_o in the mantle and core. Since by definition, in homogeneous material $k = \rho dp/d\rho$, it followed that $k \propto \rho^{\alpha}$ and hence if ρ_o is the density that the core-material would have at zero-pressure (but without change of phase), that $k/k_o = (\rho/\rho_o)^{\alpha}$, where k_o is the appropriate value for the core. Making use of known numerical values for ρ and k just inside the core-boundary (from an unstated source, however, but necessarily prior to 1949), Ramsey found that $\alpha = 3.8$, $k_o = 0.54 \times 10^{12}$ dyn/cm^2, as already quoted above, and the figure $\rho_o = 4.8$ g/cm^3 for the uncompressed density, markedly less than that of liquid iron. It was later shown by Ramsey that if the core is well mixed by convection, as the greater part of it certainly must be, then α would have a value of 3.5. Ramsey naturally enough perceived the great importance of the result that the uncompressed density turns out to be much lower than that of either iron or nickel in liquid form, and that even the value found assumes conceptually no change of phase as the pressure is reduced formally to zero, whereas if in fact the core-material were to undergo a change of structure as the pressure lowered, for instance by recovering the outer electronic shell, as would certainly occur if the core-form is a phase-change, this could only lead to decrease of the uncompressed density below the figure 4.8 g/cm^3, which value itself rules out any possibility of identification with iron or nickel.

Extensive theoretical investigation of the subject on a similar basis was carried out independently a decade or so later by Savic P. and Kasani R. in a series of little-known papers entitled The Behaviour of Materials under High Pressure, Serbian Acad. of Science & Arts, Vols 351, 1962 ; 360, 1963 ; 378, 1964 ; and 393, 1965. Their discussion takes account only of pressure-effects, with the small expansion effects of temperature shown as being equivalent to a negative pressure. It showed that with increasing pressure, at a series of critical values, material would undergo a succession of phase-changes as the structures of the electron-shells break down in turn. The maximum increase of density in any one such change was shown to be double that attainable in the previous phase. This result is not inconsistent with the interpretation of the innermost core of the Earth as a further phase-change within the liquid core, for the density at the base of the mantle is 5.68 g/cm^3, while in the liquid core just outside the inner-core boundary it is 11.54 g/cm^3, the ratio of which is not arguably different from 2 in view of the slight uncertainties associated with both values of the density.

The study appears to have been made in the absence of any knowledge of the prior work by Ramsey on the problem and makes little reference to any geophysical data, but a remarkable theorem is established which shows that the minimum mass that a spherically symmetrical gravitating body must have in order to undergo the first breakdown to the metallic phase is given by

$$M(\text{minimum}) \geqslant 9 \times 10^{29} A^{-2} \text{ gram} \quad \ldots . \ (7)$$

where A is the atomic-weight (or an appropriate mean atomic-weight) of the material of which the body is composed. This immediately shows that no such transition could occur for the Moon unless its composition were of substances with atomic-weight greater than cadmium, while Mars and Mercury would need to be almost entirely pure iron unless made up of a mixture of some of the rarer elements of comparable atomic-weight. On the other hand, for the Earth and Venus, the lower limits of A are respectively 12 and 14, so that few elements are excluded, and those are either rare or extremely light elements such as helium and hydrogen. Thus the theorem shows that both these planets could undergo the first electronic-shell breakdown to metallic form below some interior level where the pressure was sufficiently high. The result (7) is based on a single element of atomic-weight A, but for a mixture of atomic-weights A_1, A_2,....in proportions n_1, n_2,...., where $\Sigma n_r = 1$, the appropriate A can be shown to be given by $(\Sigma n_r/A_r)^{-1}$, and the foregoing conclusions for the terrestrial planets and the Moon remain substantially unchanged.

REFERENCES AND NOTES

Bell P.M. & Mao H.K. Static Generation of 1.72 Megabars Pressure, Carnegie Institution Annual Report of Geophysical Laboratory, p.908, 1977-78.

See also Reports of earlier years for the development of the diamond-anvil press and its use at lower pressures.
Since this chapter was written, successively higher pressures have been attained, the greatest so far being 1.7 x 10^{12} dyn/cm^2, and numerous phase-changes duly produced of several substances. (See the Carnegie Annual Reports for 1978-79 and 1979-80.)

Eddington A.S. Mon.Not.Roy.Astron.Soc. 77, 16, 1916.

Jeffreys H. The Earth, 1st edn, Cambridge, 1924.

Jeffreys H. The Earth, Encycl. Brit. XIVth edn, 1929.

Jeffreys H. Reports on Progress in Physics, 10,52,1945.

Kronig R.,de Boer J.,& Korringa J. Physica,12,245,1940.

This presents the theory of the phase-change of hydrogen at high pressures.

Lighthill M.J. On Instability of Small Planetary Cores, Mon.Not.Roy.Astron.Soc. 110, 339, 1950.

Lyttleton R.A. Structures of the Terrestrial Planets, Advances in Astronomy and Astrophysics, Vol.7, Academic Press, New York, 1970.

Lyttleton R.A. The Gold-Effect, Lying Truths, Pergamon, 1979.

McCrea W.H. The Study of Gravitation, Notes & Records Roy. Soc. 30(2), 133, 1976.

Oldham R.D. Quarterly Journ.Geol.Soc. 62, 456, 1906.

Paul W. & Earschauer D.M. Solids under Pressure,McGraw-Hill, 1963.

Ramsey W.H. Mon.Not.Roy.Astron.Soc. 108, 406, 1948.

Ramsey W.H. Mon.Not.Roy.Astron.Soc., Geophys. Suppl.5, 409, 1949.

Ramsey W.H. Mon.Not.Roy.Astron.Soc. 110, 325, 1950.

Ramsey W.H. Mon.Not.Roy.Astron.Soc. 110, 444, 1950.

Ramsey W.H. Mon.Not.Roy.Astron.Soc., Geophys.Suppl.6, 42, 1950.

Ramsey W.H. Occasional Notes Roy.Astron.Soc.3, 87,1954.
This is a non-technical account of the phase-change theory and related topics.

Ringwood A.E. Geochim.Cosmochim.Acta, 26, 457, 1962.

Savic P. & Kasani R. Behaviour of Materials under High Pressure, Serbian Acad.Science,351,1962; 360,1963, 378,1964; and 393,1965.
These four papers extensively develop the phase-change theory on lines similar to Ramsey's work.

6

Earth-Models Based on Seismic Data

It has been explained how Ramsey was forced to make simplifying assumptions that enabled the theory of two-zone planets to be treated mathematically, work which was done at a time when electronic computing-machines were only in the early stages of development. As has been seen, this approach restricted the conclusions to little more than results of a general order-of-magnitude nature, and in particular the possibility of a steadily contracting Earth, beyond the initial collapse, seems not to have emerged at any point in his discussions. If some actual numerical value is to be found for the rate of change of the moment-of-inertia $\dot{C}$, it is clear that more detailed consideration of the internal structure of the Earth is essential, and this is made possible by means of the known seismic data. For the purpose, the Earth can be regarded as constituted of no more than three main zones. Indeed, as earlier mentioned it is found that the relevant results are little changed if it is regarded as consisting simply of two zones, the outer one with mantle properties and the inner one having core properties. Interestingly enough, with the problem approached in this way, the Ramsey collapse duly reappears, but in a quite different manner that shows how it occurs for physical reasons.

Determination of the internal density-distribution for a given planet, as usual supposed spherically symmetrical and in equilibrium, or at relative rest at all its parts, involves finding the pressure p(r), density $\rho(r)$, and total included-mass m(r) within general distance r of the centre. Since, apart from in the surface layers, the pressure is everywhere far greater than the strength of terrestrial materials, the equation of hydrostatic equilibrium holds with high degree of accuracy, and thus

$$\frac{dp}{dr} = -g(r)\rho(r) = -\frac{Gm(r)}{r^2}\rho(r), \qquad \text{....(1)}$$

where $g(r) = Gm(r)/r^2$ is the acceleration of gravity at distance r. Next, the increment of mass for the shell from r to r + dr leads to

$$\frac{dm}{dr} = 4\pi r^2 \rho(r). \qquad \text{....(2)}$$

A third relation is therefore needed, which must depend on the physical properties of the material concerned, and this is supplied by the pressure-density relation derived from the known seismic data, which as has been seen takes the form (Ch. 2, p.42.)

$$p = \frac{a}{b}\left\{(\rho/\rho_u)^b - 1\right\} \qquad \text{....(3)}$$

wherein a, b, and ρ_u the uncompressed density, are constant within any one zone but, apart possibly from b, have different values in the different zones.

It will be convenient to associate suffixes 1, 2, 3 with the successive zones starting at the centre, so that in relation (3) the constants will be denoted as follows :

zone-1 = liquid core : a_1 b_1 $\rho_1 = \rho_u$

zone-2 = solid mantle : a_2 b_2 $\rho_2 = \rho_u$

zone-3 = outer shell : a_3 b_3 $\rho_3 = \rho_u$

The mass in the liquid core will be denoted by m_c, and in constructing a series of models it can be regarded as a parameter increasing from 0 to M the mass of the Earth or planet concerned. Now the actual Earth can of necessity have evolved with time during its history, since formation to the present, along only a single linear series of configurations, whereas if the transition from zone-2 to zone-3 were taken arbitrarily for each value of m_c, a doubly-infinite series would result. Physically, as noted in Ch. 2, this transition occurs in the Earth now at a pressure of 0.141×10^{12} dyn/cm^2, and represents a change to a denser crystal-form as a result of the pressure at that level. It would be possible to set the transition from zone-2 to zone-3 (in outward integrations) at the value of r in any model at which the pressure had fallen to this value, but, as has been seen, with increasing temperature it requires <u>higher</u> pressure to effect this particular phase-change. Thus for earlier stages, when m_c was smaller, with the Earth at generally lower temperature at corresponding parts of its interior, it would be possible to make some allowance for the effect in calculations by introducing an empirical rule relating p_{23}, the pressure at the interface between zones 2 and 3, to the growing m_c-value, and the results, to be given here have made use of the following rule relating p_{23} (with units of 10^{12} dyn/cm^2) to the corresponding mass m_c (in units of 10^{27} g)

$$p_{23} = 0.08003 + 0.0325\, m_c. \qquad \text{....(4)}$$

For the present value of the core-mass, 1.876×10^{27}g, this agrees with the known value, while the constant term figure of 0.08003 is suggested not only by experimental results but also by 2-zone models of the planet Mars, which as a much smaller and less massive body would be expected to be at lower internal temperatures than the Earth even if having the same radioactive content per unit mass. However, the mass of zone-3 for models representing the successive stages of the Earth contains only about ten per cent of the entire mass, and a different empirical law for p_{23} can be shown by calculations to have negligible effects on the main results. Indeed, if only two zones are assumed, with the mass of zone-3 included with that of zone-2, the results for the initial mass and size of the core after collapse, and for the subsequent rate and amount of contraction, and for the release of gravitational energy, are all found remarkably close to being equal to those given by 3-zone models as far as discussions of evolutionary questions are concerned.

For the central zone, if from (1) the pressure p is eliminated in favour of the density ρ by means of (3), and then m(r) eliminated by means of (2), it is readily found, denoting the central density by ρ_0, that if

$$\rho = \rho_0 y^n \quad \text{where } n = (b-1)^{-1} \qquad \ldots.(5)$$

then

$$\frac{d^2y}{dr^2} + \frac{2}{r}\frac{dy}{dr} + \frac{4\pi G\rho_1^{\,b}}{na\rho_0^{\,b-2}}\, y^n = 0. \qquad \ldots.(6)$$

If r is now replaced by the dimensionless variable x defined by

$$r^2 = \frac{na\rho_0^{\,b-2}}{4\pi G\rho_1^{\,b}}\, x^2 = L^2x^2, \qquad \ldots.(7)$$

thereby introducing a standard length L associated with the system, then (6) takes dimensionless form, which has the advantage of keeping the needed calculations to a minimum, namely

$$\frac{d^2y}{dx^2} + \frac{2}{x}\frac{dy}{dx} + y^n = 0. \qquad \ldots.(8)$$

This is the Emden-equation of order n, well known in the theory of stellar structure. It can be shown readily that the distribution in each zone depends on an Emden-equation, but if calculations using different values of b in the several zones are made (which has been done, though the results are not included here), then the value of n will be slightly different in the zones in accordance with its definition as $(b-1)^{-1}$.

In the present problem, as has been seen, b is close to 3.5 in each zone and thus n is always close to 0.4, and in all cases (5) is a non-linear second-order equation. Its solutions in general possess a singularity (an infinity) at $x = 0$, but it also has a unique solution well-behaved at $x = 0$, which can be expressed near $x = 0$ as a convergent series in powers of x with initial terms

$$y = 1 - \frac{1}{6}x^2 + \frac{n}{120}x^4 - \ldots., \qquad \ldots.(9)$$

and this solution is of utmost importance to the planetary problems since it satisfies the relevant physical conditions at the centre. For near the centre, the pressure-gradient

$$dp/dr \rightarrow -\frac{4}{3}\pi G\rho_o^{\,2}r \rightarrow 0 \text{ as } r \rightarrow 0, \qquad \ldots.(10)$$

since ρ_o for physical reasons must clearly be finite at the centre. Hence by (3), $d\rho/dr \rightarrow 0$, which in turn means that $dy/dx = 0$ at $x = 0$. Also, by (5), it is necessary that $y = 1$ at $x = 0$. Thus the appropriate solution is that corresponding to (9), which is a solution free from any singularity at $x = 0$ that a general solution of the equation would necessarily possess. Thus only by integrating outwards from the centre can the possibility be avoided of the solution diverging as the centre of the planet is approached. In the other zones, the value of r does not vanish, and no possibility of encountering any singularity therein arises.

In conducting the calculations, the value of the central density is not known to begin with, and some reasonable value has to be adopted : integration is then made step-by-step from the centre using the values a_1, b_1, ρ_1 until m(r) has reached the selected value m_c of the core-mass. The values a_2, b_2, ρ_2 now take over in (3) for zone-2, while the conditions for the continuity of pressure and gravity across the interface supply new starting-values for the density and its gradient at the inner boundary of zone-2. The integration can then be continued outward until the pressure has fallen to the value given by (4) for the initially adopted m_c. Again, continuity of pressure and gravity provide commencing values for the integration in zone-3 using a_3, b_3, ρ_3. If with the selected ρ_0, the pressure has not vanished before reaching zone-3 and the interior mass m(r) has not reached M the total mass of the planet, then in zone-3, either p(r) will vanish before M has been encompassed, or m(r) will reach M before p(r) has vanished. In either event, a physically possible model has clearly not been reached. A different starting value for ρ_0, the central density, must therefore be adopted, and the outward integration repeated. By means of an interpolation-procedure within the computer program, the appropriate value of ρ_0 can soon be found with any desired degree of accuracy, and then integration will reach p(r) = 0, the surface, at precisely the value of r for which m(r) = M, and incidentally provide the whole march of properties from centre to surface, in particular the pressure at the interface between zones 1 and 2, the core-radius, and the density distribution with r. The value of r at which p(r) = 0 and m(r) = M will of course be the surface-radius r_s for the model of core-mass m_c.

For two-zone models of the Earth (or other planet), p_{23} vanishes, as it is now the surface-pressure, and no empirical rule such as (1) is needed. Once m_c is assigned, the interface $r = r_c$ between zones 1 and 2 has simply to be selected, by interpolation to the appropriate ρ_0 as before so that p(r) reaches zero in zone 2 at the same value of $r = r_s$ for which m(r) reaches M.

By these means, the results set out in Table 8 for

3-zone models of the Earth, and in Table 9 for 2-zone models, have been obtained. The symbols adopted for the various relevant quantities are as follows :

m_c = adopted mass of core,

r_c = radius of liquid core, $m(r_c) = m_c$,

ρ_o = central density,

p_o = central pressure,

p_{12} = pressure at interface between zones 1 & 2,

r_m = radius to outer boundary of mantle (zone-2),

p_{23} = pressure at interface between zones 2 & 3,

m_{12} = combined mass of zones 1 & 2 = $m(r_m)$,

r_s = surface-radius : i.e. $p(r_s) = 0$, $m(r_s) = M$,

C = moment-of-inertia about any diameter (not tabulated) = Mfr_s^2,

f = moment-of-inertia factor = C/Mr_s^2, ($f = 0.4$ for a uniform sphere),

fr_s^2 = moment-of-inertia per unit mass of model,

$-W$ = total exhaustion of gravitational energy of the distribution (with zero corresponding to infinite dispersion),

ρ_m = mean-density of entire model = $3M/4\pi r_s^3$.

For the series of 2-zone models, r_m becomes equal to the surface-radius, p_{23} vanishes, and m_{12} is the total mass of the planet ; these are therefore not listed in Table 9.

In regard to both Tables, it will be appreciated that in deriving the results, numerical values for the constants a, b, ρ_u in each zone once adopted must henceforth be regarded as completely accurate, even though derived from values for physical quantities (the seismic data) having at most 3-figure accuracy. Nor would it make any important difference to the final results if slightly different values for the constants were used so long as these were again regarded as completely accurate. As the equations are non-linear, it is necessary in the computations to carry a larger number of decimal places than the original three significant figures in the individual values of k, p, and ρ at different levels in the Earth as given in Table 3, Chap.2. If only three figures were retained at every step, no results of any value would emerge because of rapidly-growing numerical errors, as is of course well known in computing theory. In the calculations on which the results given were based, at least eight figures were always retained, and several more in a few runs to make certain of the reliability of these, but in Tables 8 and 9 five and sometimes only four figures are given for the sake of economy of space. The necessity for a larger number of figures (than 3) is illustrated by the values for W, for which only the differences can enter physically, since its zero can be fixed arbitrarily and need not refer to infinite dispersion (the zero adopted here). The value of W is seen to change only slightly along the series from $m_c = 0$ to $m_c = 1.876 \times 10^{27}$ g the present value, while the difference between its values for $m_c = 0$ and $m_c = 0.3708 \times 10^{27}$ g (the energy released in the collapse) is readily found from Table I to be 0.00594×10^{40} erg. Thus at least five figures would obviously be needed in the integrations leading to W in order to end up with three significant figures, and in fact more are needed in the quantities involved. Where evolutionary questions are concerned, it is <u>differences</u> mainly of quantities for different values of m_c that enter, and these turn out to be much the same numerically whether the values of Table 8 or Table 9 are used.

TABLE 8 : THREE-ZONE MODELS OF THE EARTH

m_c (10^{27}g)	ρ_o (g cm^{-3})	p_o (10^{12} cgs)	r_c (km)	p_{12} (10^{12} cgs)	r_m (km)	p_{23} (10^{12} cgs)	m_{12} (10^{27} g)	r_s (km)	f	fr_s^2 (10^{18} cm^2)	$-W$ (10^{40} erg)	ρ_m (g cm^{-3})
0	(5.76)											
$0.0^{10}1$	10.06	1.6337	1.3	1.6337	6472.6	0.0800	5.474	6741.5	0.3783	0.1719	0.21802	4.656
0.05	10.30	1.8092	1054.9	1.6471	6458.7	0.0817	5.467	6732.2	0.3767	0.1707	0.21882	4.676
0.1	10.44	1.9101	1326.6	1.6495	6444.9	0.0833	5.460	6722.8	0.3752	0.1696	0.21962	4.695
0.15	10.54	1.9940	1516.5	1.6493	6431.1	0.0849	5.454	6713.3	0.3737	0.1684	0.22042	4.715
0.2	10.64	2.0685	1667.1	1.6473	6417.2	0.0865	5.447	6703.9	0.3723	0.1673	0.22122	4.735
0.25	10.72	2.1367	1794.0	1.6443	6403.4	0.0882	5.441	6694.4	0.3709	0.1662	0.22202	4.755
0.3	10.80	2.2002	1904.7	1.6404	6389.6	0.0898	5.434	6684.9	0.3694	0.1651	0.22282	4.776
0.35	10.87	2.2600	2003.5	1.6358	6375.8	0.0914	5.428	6675.4	0.3681	0.1640	0.22362	4.796
0.3708	10.90	2.2836	2041.9	1.6337	6370.1	0.0921	5.426	6671.4	0.3675	0.1636	0.22396	4.80[illegible]
0.4	10.93	2.317	2093.1	1.631	6362.0	0.0930	5.422	6665.8	0.3667	0.1629	0.22442	4.817
0.5	11.06	2.423	2251.8	1.619	6334.5	0.0963	5.410	6646.6	0.3641	0.1609	0.22602	4.859
1.0	11.53	2.865	2825.4	1.539	6197.6	0.1125	5.359	6549.0	0.3552	0.1510	0.23387	5.079
1.5	11.87	3.218	3226.8	1.435	6062.0	0.1288	5.318	6448.6	0.3522	0.1423	0.24138	5.321
1.876	12.08	3.448	3476.7	1.348	5960.7	0.141	5.295	6371.2	0.3422	0.1363	0.24678	5.516
2.0	12.15	3.517	3551.7	1.317	5927.5	0.1450	5.288	6345.3	0.3340	0.1345	0.24850	5.584
3.0	12.55	3.991	4076.0	1.040	5660.9	0.1775	5.257	6129.4	0.3238	0.1216	0.26107	6.196
4.0	12.82	4.326	4516.8	0.7217	5396.1	0.2100	5.260	5899.5	0.3227	0.1123	0.27094	6.948
5.0	12.98	4.532	4925.0	0.3672	5131.0	0.2425	5.292	5654.4	0.3333	0.1066	0.27741	7.892
5.3	13.00	4.567	5047.4	0.2548	5051.5	0.2523	5.306	5577.9	0.3393	0.1056	0.27857	8.221

Earth : $M = 5.976 \times 10^{27}$g, $b = 3.5$ throughout, $p_{23} = 0.08003 + 0.0325 m_c$.

core $\begin{cases} a_1 = 1.3416 \times 10 \text{ cgs}, \\ \rho_1 = 6.26 \text{ g cm}^{-3} \end{cases}$ mantle $\begin{cases} a_2 = 2.1505 \times 10^{12} \text{ cgs} \\ \rho_2 = 3.975 \text{ g cm}^{-3} \end{cases}$ outer shell $\begin{cases} a_3 = 1.1673 \times 10^{12} \text{ cgs} \\ \rho_3 = 3.298 \text{ g cm}^{-3} \end{cases}$

TABLE 9 : TWO-ZONE MODELS OF THE EARTH

m_c (10^{27} g)	ρ_0 (g cm^{-3})	p_0 (10^{12} cgs)	r_c (km)	p_{12} (10^{12} cgs)	r_s (km)	f	fr_s^2 (10^{18} cm^2)	$-W$ (10^{40} erg)	ρ_m (g cm^{-3})
0.0	(5.922)								
0.0+	10.23	1.6944	+0.0	1.6944	6644.9	0.3823	0.1688	0.22003	4.863
0.05	10.47	1.8723	1049.2	1.7067	6635.1	0.3808	0.1676	0.22082	4.884
0.1	10.60	1.9745	1319.6	1.7083	6625.3	0.3793	0.1665	0.22162	4.906
0.15	10.71	2.0594	1508.5	1.7073	6615.5	0.3779	0.1654	0.22242	4.928
0.2	10.80	2.1348	1658.4	1.7047	6605.6	0.3765	0.1643	0.22322	4.950
0.25	10.89	2.2038	1784.6	1.7011	6595.8	0.3752	0.1632	0.22402	4.972
0.3	10.96	2.2680	1894.8	1.6966	6585.9	0.3739	0.1622	0.22482	4.994
0.3215	11.00	2.2940	1938.5	1.6944	6581.6	0.3733	0.1617	0.22516	5.004
0.35	11.04	2.328	1993.1	1.691	6576.0	0.3725	0.1611	0.22562	5.017
0.4	11.10	2.386	2082.4	1.686	6566.1	0.3713	0.1601	0.22642	5.040
0.5	11.22	2.493	2240.4	1.673	6546.2	0.3687	0.1580	0.22801	5.086
1.0	11.70	2.940	2811.6	1.587	6445.6	0.3754	0.1485	0.23582	5.328
1.5	12.04	3.296	3211.4	1.479	6343.1	0.3479	0.1400	0.24330	5.591
1.876	12.25	3.527	3460.3	1.387	6264.7	0.3419	0.1342	0.24865	5.803
2.0	12.32	3.597	3535.1	1.355	6238.5	0.3401	0.1324	0.25035	5.876
3.0	12.72	4.073	4057.6	1.070	6022.3	0.3306	0.1199	0.26281	6.532
4.0	12.99	4.410	4497.0	0.743	5795.2	0.3302	0.1109	0.27256	7.330
5.0	13.14	4.617	4904.0	0.380	5555.8	0.3413	0.1053	0.27894	8.316
5.976	13.19	4.686	5312.6	0.0	5312.6	0.3667	0.1035	0.28115	9.515

Earth : $M = 5.976 \times 10^{27}$ g, $b = 3.5$ throughout, $p_{23} = 0.$

core $\begin{cases} a_1 = 1.3416 \times 10^{12} \text{ cgs} \\ \rho_1 = 6.31 \text{ g cm}^{-3} \end{cases}$ mantle $\begin{cases} a_2 = 2.1505 \times 10^{12} \text{ cgs} \\ \rho_2 = 4.057 \text{ g cm}^{-3} \end{cases}$

Also, the geometrical properties of a sphere are involved if only implicitly, and it is important to recognise that these follow far-from-linear rules. To illustrate this, if a uniform solid sphere the size of the Earth were to undergo an increase of outer radius by a mere 1 km, without change of density anywhere, at the expense of creating a spherical hollow at the centre, this hollow would have radius 496 km. An increase by 2 km would produce a hollow 625 km in radius, not double the first value. Reversely, if such a sphere were decreased in radius by 1 km, this could be achieved by doubling the density in a central sphere of 496 km radius, immediately suggestive of the 'large core' after collapse found by Ramsey, who estimated that the outer radius of the Earth would decrease by about 100 km in the collapse, and this if achieved by doubling the density of a central core would give it a radius of nearly 2300 km.

In Tables 8 & 9, the central density shown in brackets for $m_c = 0$ refers to the case where there is no liquid core and the solid mantle extends down to the centre, while the other value shown is for an infinitesimal liquid core, $m_c = +0$. For the 3-zone series, their ratio $10.06/5.76 = 1.75$ is the value of λ, and for the 2-zone series it is seen to be $10.23/5.92 = 1.73$. Thus for both series, λ is substantially greater than the critical value 1.5, and the Ramsey collapse will therefore occur.

In regard to the results of Tables 8 and 9, it will be understood in the light of the discussion of the phase-change theory in Chap.5 that although each line of values in the Tables gives the principal physical quantities associated with a model of selected core-mass with all its elements at rest, it is not necessarily the case that the particular distribution would be a possible static-equilibrium model. As will become clear below, the 3-zone models with $m_c < 0.3708 \times 10^{27}$ g and the 2-zone models with $m_c < 0.3215 \times 10^{27}$ g come into such a category and although at rest do not represent models in equilibrium. The bead on the wire (Fig. 5, page 97.) supplies a simple analogy to the present situation in that once the system reaches the curve 55, the bead can nevertheless be regarded as conceptually at rest at any point of the wire between AB and C, and it will have a definite potential energy and reaction on the wire for its position. But until the bead reaches C, the force acting on it would not maintain it in equilibrium whatever amount of friction (proportional to the velocity) were involved. In the same way, although conceptual models can be calculated corresponding to points of YY' in Fig. 6, page 99, they cannot represent physically possible static-equilibrium models.

The first feature of importance in Table 8 for 3-zone models to which it is wished to draw attention arises from the values of the pressure p_{12} at the core-mantle boundary. When $m_C = 0$, this is of course also the central pressure, which is 1.6377×10^{12} dyn/cm^2. It will be recalled that for a planet of constant mass, the phase-change waits on rising temperature, and the Ramsey-collapse commences only when the critical temperature is reached associated with a given pressure. It has also been seen that the central regions of the Earth, and indeed far beyond, remain isothermal though increasing in temperature with time as a result of radioactive energy-release. Also with $m_C = 0$, the pressure everywhere decreases outwards, as equation (1) shows, and therefore the phase-change would set in only at the centre when the prevailing temperature had risen to the critical value. But the moment the change of phase occurs in however small an element of volume at the centre, the value of m_C immediately rises above zero, and the remarkable result emerges from Table 1 that p_{12}, the pressure at the extreme base of zone-2, is now higher than the original central value $p_0(m_C=0)$. Thus to begin with, as m_C increases so does p_{12}. But the solid material at the inner boundary of. zone-2 is already at sufficient temperature for the phase-change to occur if the pressure were only equal to $p_0(m_C = 0)$, and therefore the existing pressure is more than adequate. Thus more material of zone-2 undergoes the phase-change to liquid form, and m_C therefore continues to increase. This is illustrated schematically in Fig.8.

The values of p_{12} in Table 8 show that (in units of 10^{12} cgs) this interface-pressure starts at 1.6337,

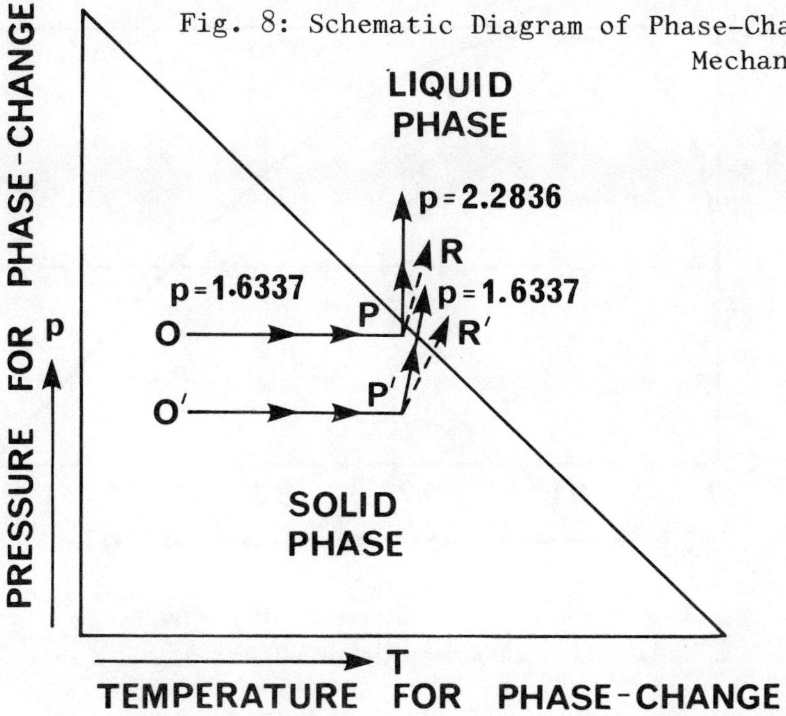

Fig. 8: Schematic Diagram of Phase-Change Mechanism

rises to a maximum of 1.6496, and then decreases monotonically with increasing m_c to fall back to the original central pressure of 1.6337 for $m_c = 0.3708 \times 10^{27}$g. Thus it is to be emphasised that during these stages the pressure at the base of the solid mantle will be more than sufficient to bring about the phase-change, which will continue to occur until a liquid core with mass 0.3708×10^{27}g has formed and the pressure at its boundary has fallen back to the original central value of 1.6337×10^{12} dyn/cm^2 associated with with $m_c = 0$ (see Fig. 9). Once the temperature has risen to the critical value associated with the central pressure in the all-solid planet, the static models are no longer physically possible equilibrium configurations. Dynamical motion will therefore set in (the Ramsey collapse) and the planet move rapidly through the series from $m_c=0$ to $m_c = 0.3708 \times 10^{27}$dyn/cm^2. This is how the Ramsey-collapse manifests itself when the problem is treated by making use of the seismic data in the present way.

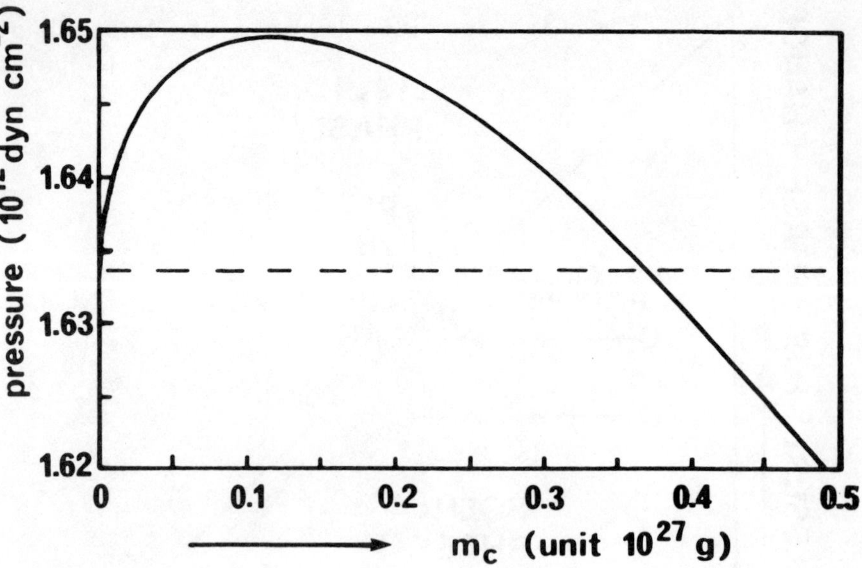

Fig. 9
Showing the initial <u>increase</u> of pressure p_{12} at the core-mantle boundary.

Of course in reality, since $p_{12} > p(\text{critical})$ during the collapse, this motion would be almost certain to overshoot the mark at which $m_c = 0.3708 \times 10^{27}$g and where $p_{12} = 1.6337 \times 10^{12}$dyn/cm². If this did occur, p_{12} would soon become <u>less</u> than the original p_o, and the conditions at the base of zone-2 no longer suitable for further phase-change. On the other hand, the system could conceptually be brought very slowly to the configuration with $m_c = 0.3708 \times 10^{27}$g by supposing p_{12} somehow constrained to remain always only minutely greater than 1.6337×10^{12} dyn/cm². The system would then come to rest in equilibrium with $m_c = 0.3798 \times 10^{27}$g, though this would require work to be done to maintain velocities always at nearly zero. This collapsed configuration corresponds to point Y' of Fig. 6, p. 99.), and as seen from Table 8 has core-radius 2042 km, a 'large radius' as predicted by Ramsey, but now with a specific value found for it on the basis of the seismic data. Since this core-mass is just under one-fifth of the present value, 1.876×10^{27}/g, it is plain that this initial core cannot possibly be identified with the existing core, which has radius 3473 km, and therefore that further considerable evolution of the planet along the series Y'Q must have taken place since the collapse. But for $m_c > 0.3708 \times 10^{27}$g, the interface-pressure p_{12} is always less than the original central pressure just before and at the onset of the phase-change, and accordingly further evolution after the collapse must wait on gradual rise of temperature through radioactivity to offset the lower pressure. The Earth will thus evolve steadily along an equilibrium series Y'Q thoroughly stable at every stage, the rate of evolution depending on the rate of rise of temperature and its relation to the phase-change. Column-9 in Table 8 for r_s shows that the overall radius of the planet decreases steadily as the series is followed with gradually increasing m_c. The moment of inertia per unit mass, and thus the moment of inertia itself, also decreases with increasing m_c, and as would be expected, the moment-of-inertia factor f also decreases as the degree of central concentration of mass increases.

Table 9 gives the corresponding results for the simpler case of 2-zone models consisting of a liquid core and a surrounding solid mantle only. Just as for the 3-zone series, the pressure p_{12} at the interface at first increases as the core-mass increases from zero, and then returns to the original central value $p_0(m_c = 0)$ when $m_c = 0.3215 \times 10^{27}$g, showing again how the Ramsey-collapse presents itself when the seismic data are used. Beyond the collapse-stage, for greater m_c, the planet is thoroughly stable, and would evolve along the series corresponding to Y'Q with rising internal temperature. The overall radius r_s again decreases along the series, as also does the moment-of-inertia Mfr_s^2, and also the factor f. These 2-zone models are systematically smaller than the 3-zone models at corresponding values of m_c by about 100 km in radius. This clearly is the result of the outer-shell material, which has an uncompressed density of about 3.3g/cm^3, being included as if it were mantle-material of uncompressed density slightly greater than 4 g/cm^3.

It is of interest to notice that the <u>differences</u> of values of individual properties along the two series are all nearly equal numerically. Thus for the 3-zone series, the gravitational energy released in the collapse, which is found from the column for $-W$, is 5.94×10^{37} erg, and after the collapse to the present stage ($m_C = 1.876 \times 10^{27}$ g) is 2.282×10^{38} erg, making a total energy-release of 2.876×10^{38} erg. Corresponding figures for the 2-zone series, from the values of $-W$ in Table 9 are 5.13×10^{37} erg during collapse, 2.349×10^{38} erg after that to the present, giving a total of 2.862×10^{38} erg. Where the moment-of-inertia is concerned, it is seen that for both series this has decreased by almost the same factor (0.83) from immediately after the collapse to the present value of m_C, while the actual decrease for the same range is $2.724 \times 10^{16}\,cm^2$ per unit mass in the 3-zone series, and $2.753 \times 10^{16}\,cm^2$ per unit mass in the 2-zone series, an entirely unimportant difference. For the purpose of later discussion the 3-zone series will be used, but the very slight differences of these main properties, especially of the moments-of-inertia when the outer-shell material is included with the mantle, which is equivalent to assuming $p_{23} = 0$, brings out the point that any reasonable empirical law for p_{23}, for a 3-zone series slightly different from that used, equation (4), would only alter the results by negligible amounts, and this has been verified to be the case by numerous calculations, not included here for reasons of space, based on other empirical relations for p_{23} in terms of m_C.

As will be discussed in some detail later, the steady decrease of r_s along the series is of utmost importance where the theory of mountain-building is concerned, but the property of special relevance to the theory of tidal friction (Chap.4) is the moment of inertia $C = Mfr_s^{\,2}$, which is seen to diminish substantially as the core-mass increases. What is required for comparison with the tidal-friction results is an independent determination of a numerical value for $\dot{C}$ more or less at the present time, that is over about the past 3000 years covered by the ancient-eclipse data. A degree of uncertainty enters in making use of the foregoing calculated values of fr_s^2 because the most that can at present be extracted is clearly only the average time-rate of decrease of C since the collapse. This requires some estimate of the instant in the past at which collapse occurred, and the range of -4.0×10^9 years to -2.5×10^9 years ago would seem to be certain to include the crucial time. Indeed, it turns out that any value within this range enables adequate accuracy to be achieved for the purposes of comparison with the results for tidal-friction theory, and in particular for deriving the fictitious couple $-\omega\dot{C}$ from the values of fr_s^2. The <u>change</u> of fr_s^2 for the 3-zone series from the time of collapse to the present ($m_C = 1.876 \times 10^{27}$g) is seen to be $0.0273 \times 10^{18}\text{cm}^2$, while on the 2-zone series it is negligibly different at $0.0275 \times 10^{18}\text{cm}^2$, and it will therefore suffice to adopt the 3-zone figure. Then for a series of assumed values for the instant of collapse, spaced half an aeon apart, the time average of $-\omega\dot{C}$ and the corresponding values of $\dot{\omega}_i/\omega$ can be readily found, and are as follows :

TABLE 10

Time of collapse τ (10^9 years)	$-\omega\dot{C}$ (on Table 8) (cgs units)	$\dot{\omega}_i/\omega$ (10^{-11}/yr)
- 4.0	0.94×10^{23}	5.06
- 3.5	1.07×10^{23}	5.78
- 3.0	1.25×10^{23}	6.75
- 2.5	1.50×10^{23}	8.10

These may be compared with the values determined from tidal-friction theory (Chap.4,p.82), which were :

Linear friction : $\dot{\omega}_i/\omega = 6.23 \times 10^{-11}$/yr,

Quadratic friction : $\dot{\omega}_i/\omega = 7.57 \times 10^{-11}$/yr.

On these figures, agreement with linear friction would require a time of collapse $\tau = -3.2 \times 10^9$ yr, and with quadratic friction -2.7×10^9 years ago. Thus it emerges that for about the first 1.5×10^9 years of its existence, the Earth remained in all-solid form, at least in its central regions, with the central temperature gradually rising all the time before reaching the critical value for the onset of the phase-change.

The closeness of fit stands out even more strikingly if the results are displayed in graphical form (Fig. 10). Equation (30) of Chap.4 may for this purpose be written in the form

$$N'(\text{tidal}) - \omega C(\dot{\omega}_i/\omega) = 0.15 \pm 0.44 \qquad \text{....(11)}$$

in units of 10^{23}cgs, the derivation having been made on the basis of constant G. (The effect of a "constant of gravitation" changing with time will be considered in Chapter 9). With N' (in units of 10^{23}cgs) as ordinate, and $\dot{\omega}_i/\omega$ (in units of 10^{-11}/yr) as abscissa, equation (11) leads to a straight line sloping up to the right, as shown in Fig.10, and two lines parallel to this have been drawn at distances above and below it equal to the standard error $\pm$ 0.44. The value of N'(tidal) with its error-range, follows by scaling from the lunar tidal couple $(4.74 \pm 0.38) \times 10^{23}$cgs found in Chap.4 with due allowance for the thermal contribution. There will be two cases : first for linear tidal friction, and second for quadratic friction. These with their error-ranges will give two narrow horizontal bands, shown as $N'(\text{linear}) = 1.00 \pm 0.08$, and $N'(\text{quadratic}) = 1.25 \pm 0.10$ in the diagram, and any point within the heavy-lined parallelogram-shaped areas will give a solution satisfying tidal-friction theory and lying within the error-limits. For a solution to be satisfactory, its representative-point must also correspond to a value of $\dot{\omega}_i/\omega$ consistent with the geophysical requirement imposed by a contracting Earth. The vertical lines correspond to times of collapse τ at -4.0, -3.5, -3.0, and -2.5 aeons. For friction entirely linear, the diagram shows that for the representative-point to remain

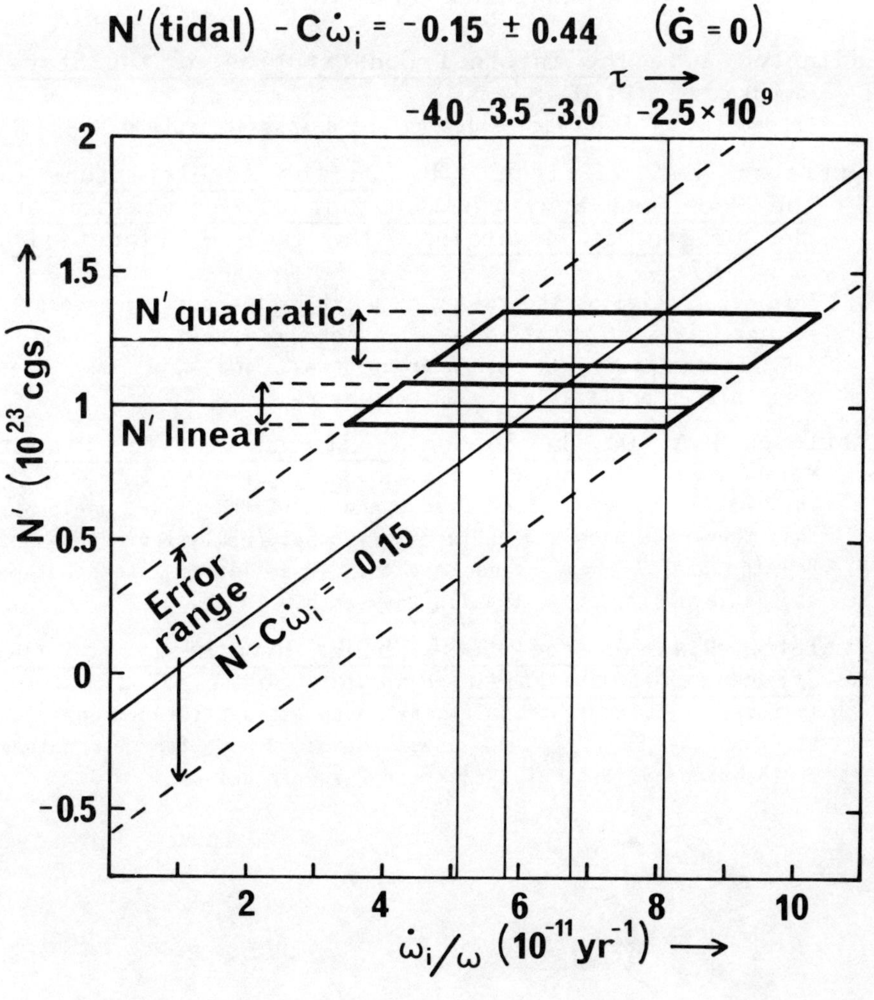

Fig. 10

within the parallelogram, τ can range from about -3.5 to -3.1 aeons, while for purely quadratic friction τ can range from about -2.9 to -2.5 aeons. If the actual friction is a combination of both kinds, then some intermediate range such as -3.0 ± 0.2 aeons could well be appropriate.

REFERENCES AND NOTES

Eddington A.S. The Internal Constitution of the Stars, Cambridge, 1930.

Properties of the Emden-equation are discussed in Chap.4.

Lyttleton R.A. & Fitch J.P. On the Accelerations of the Moon and Sun, the Constant of Gravitation and the Origin of Mountains, The Moon & Planets, 18, 223, 1978.

This paper develops the theory by which Earth-models are computed and gives a detailed example in the Appendix, p.238. Dr J.P. Fitch wrote the computer-programs, and will make them available on application by anyone interested.

Lyttleton R.A. On the Internal Structure of the Planet Mars. Mon.Not.Roy.Astron.Soc. 129, 21, 1965.

This paper gives detailed 2-zone models of the planet and shows that the known mass and radius imply considerable lower pressure for the Bernal phase-change and thus lower internal temperature at the level it occurs than in the Earth.

Lyttleton R.A. On the Phase-Change Hypothesis for the Structure of the Earth, Proc.Roy.Soc.A 287, 471, 1965.

In this paper, contraction of the Earth was predicted theoretically on the basis of the phase-change theory for the nature of the core by means of 3-zone and 2-zone models.

7

The Origin of Mountains

It has been seen how the terrestrial planets and the Moon will have begun their existences as all-solid bodies after practically the whole of the material of the original dust-disc in their realms had been gathered in to form them. Once having reached that stage, there would be no further mechanism to bring about evolution were it not for their comparatively small content of the long-lived radioactive elements, which leads to gradually rising internal temperature everywhere except to a minute extent at the free surface. As a result, the level corresponding to the (present) 20°-discontinuity would move slightly deeper to achieve the greater pressure needed for this phase-change with rising temperature, and through conversion back to the less-dense crystal form of some of the mantle-material, the Earth would expand very slightly.

Only for the Earth (and Venus, as will be shown) is the central pressure high enough for the temperature to have reached the critical value needed for the phase change to metallic liquid form. The seismic data show that the crucial factor λ, measuring the density-jump, is in fact considerably greater than 1.5 and the Ramsey collapse will therefore occur. The actual value, $\lambda = 1.75$, must be a property of terrestrial material in the different phases at this pressure and temperature, but even if λ happened to be less than about 1.5 (but greater than unity), evolution would still occur after the critical temperature was reached accompanied by contraction of the planet as a whole, but with the essential difference that there would be no sudden collapse. Instead, the mass and radius of the core would increase continuously from zero, and the outer radius decrease steadily. The sudden collapse for the actual Earth may however have important consequences of special relevance to the production of continents, the materials of which are known to have markedly less density than the average uncompressed density of the present outer 413 km at 3.3 g/cm^3.

Referring to Fig. 7, p.105, this was seen to represent schematically the rising temperature-distribution, T(r,t) say, within the Earth as a result of radioactive heating, and also the melting-point temperatures with depth and with distance from the centre. Since every volume-element must on average release the same amount of radioactive energy per unit mass, and conduction of heat proceeds so extremely slowly, it follows from calculations that almost the whole of the interior has the same uniform though rising temperature at any time t, and only in a shallow layer near the surface does a temperature-gradient come to exist whereby the temperature declines to the fixed surface-value of about 300K. With increasing internal temperature, this outer layer in which the gradient -dT/dr differs importantly from zero, gradually reaches to greater depth. As the interior remains isothermal, but with steadily rising temperature, the distribution of T with r at any stage will be represented by a straight line. Now it has been seen that at pressures sufficiently low the solid-phase has density greater than the liquid-phase, the melting-point temperature <u>increases</u> with depth, and, as may be seen from Fig. 7, p.105, the rising internal temperature curve could eventually become tangential to the melting-point curve at a place of some moderate depth such as M_S. If this should occur <u>before</u> the central temperature has reached that necessary for the onset of the Ramsey-collapse, then the temperature distribution curve, still rising, will cross above the melting-point curve, and a spherical shell of material between certain depths will become molten but remain confined both above and below by boundaries of material still in solid form. Being in liquid form, the materials will undergo stratification as a result of gravity, with the lightest materials rising to the top, the density increasing downwards, and the heaviest sinking to the bottom in accordance with the requirements of hydrostatic equilibrium.

It is a well-known theorem that, for a spherical distribution in hydrostatic equilibrium, any such rearrangement of mass, with lighter materials transferred outwards and heavier ones inwards, will increase the central pressure, and thus in the present case will lower the requisite critical central temperature, say T_c, for the phase-change. But there would be no reason to suppose that T_c would be reached just at the time that the T(r,t)-curve comes into contact with the melting point curve. If T_c is reached before that, no shallow molten layer would have formed, and the present considerations would be irrelevant to the development of the Earth at that stage. On the other hand, if T_c is reached <u>after</u> this first contact, the resulting slight increase of central pressure would slightly reduce T_c, and cause the onset of collapse to occur a little earlier than otherwise. The collapse itself would have been of an almost inconceivably catastrophic nature by any terrestrial standards, involving the sudden release of some 5.94×10^{37} ergs of energy (Table 8, Chap. 6), which is about 10^{13} times the energy of the yet greatest known earthquakes, not to mention the accompanying decrease of outer radius by 70km. As to the details of how it would take place, they defy the imagination to envisage. Certainly it would be unlikely to occur with spherical symmetry. Signs of the final stages of growth of the Moon by infall of large objects are still to be seen as the giant maria, and it must be the case that the growth of the Earth involved infall of at least equally large bodies and on average with greater energy per unit mass through the stronger terrestrial attraction. Such impacts, besides producing large craters, would assuredly sunder the surface layers by causing cracks and fissures extending to great distances from the craters themselves. These already-existing lines of weakness would be sites automatically available for the violent adjustments that must take place. Since radial collapse by an average of 70 km will be the final outcome, any molten layer not unduly far below the surface would be likely to have its outer solid boundary heavily breached in places, and hydrostatic forces are so strong that the lighter molten material would well up to the surface through the channels so created. This then describes a possible mechanism whereby this less dense material could come to be spread over parts of the surface to form continents, for once such an escape-cleft to the free surface was established, further light molten material would be driven to its base, squeezed down and forced there more or less horizontally by the collapsing solid material originally above it. The continents are known to be fairly deep-rooted, extending down some 50-70 km for the most part.

The time required for the main stage of this cataclysmic collapse would have been extremely short, as Ramsey emphasised, being "comparable with the time taken for free fall of a particle through 100 km, (his estimate of the decrease of outer radius) under gravity: that is, a matter of minutes", and he added, "or at most hours" in view of the possibility of heavy dissipation. The total gravitational energy released will be disposed of in three main ways : First, a small proportion will reappear as an increase of kinetic energy of rotation, since the angular momentum of the planet remains constant while the moment-of-inertia decreases. Second, work will be done in compressing the part of the Earth that remains solid as the mantle (and outer-shell) and be stored in the form of elastic energy. Third, which is the overwhelming proportion, work will be done on the material that becomes the liquid core and be stored there as the major part of the energy possessed by the material in its changed phase, with also the earlier accumulated heat of radioactive energy and other minor sources. To calculate numerical values for these, it is simpler to use the 2-zone series of models, particularly where the elastic energy of the mantle is concerned. On this basis, the total energy to be disposed in the collapse is now 5.13×10^{37}erg, (by Table 9).

If just before the onset, the rotation period $2\pi/\omega$ of the Earth were 5 hours, to take a round figure, then since the angular momentum $C\omega = H$, say, it will be conserved in the collapse, therefore the rotatory energy $\frac{1}{2}C\omega^2 = H^2/2C$ will increase as a result of the decrease of C. With the values of Table 2, the change is readily found to be 0.27×10^{37} erg. If the adopted initial period were longer, the change of energy would be reduced in proportion with ω^2, so the present estimate probably represents a maximum, and is only about 5 per cent of the total energy available.

Since the mass of core so produced is 0.322×10^{27}g, the mass in solid mantle-form will be 5.654×10^{27}g (by Table 9), and it would be this mass that undergoes elastic compression without change of phase during the collapse. The work needed to be done can readily be calculated by making use of the relation of pressure to density

$$p = \frac{a}{b}\left\{(\rho/\rho_u)^b - 1\right\} \qquad \ldots.(1)$$

with the values of a and ρ_u appropriate to the 2-zone models and b = 3.5. If a system (here the solid mantle) of material satisfying relation (1) undergoes a compressional change from state A to state B, then the work done by the pressure, and hence the additional energy given to it, may be shown to be equal to

$$\int_A^B (p + a)(b - 1)^{-1}\, dv \qquad \ldots.(2)$$

where dv is an infinitesimal volume-element of the material, the integral being taken through the whole of the mantle-material. This expression readily integrates and for the 2-zone series yields

$$\frac{2}{15}\left[W(r_s) - W(r_c) + 4\pi a(r_s{}^3 - r_c{}^3) - 4\pi p(r_c)r_c{}^3\right]_A^B \qquad \ldots.(3)$$

where $-W(r)$ denotes (the exhaustion of) gravitational energy of the sphere of material within distance r of the centre. The numerical value of this expression may readily be calculated for the 2-zone series of models and is found to be 1.24×10^{37} erg.

Allowing for the change of rotatory energy, 0.27×10^{37} erg, there remains energy of amount 3.62×10^{37}erg that will go to doing work on the core-material. Since the initial core-mass is 0.3215×10^{27}g, this total represents an average of 11.3×10^{10}erg/g. As radioactive heating during the approximate 1.5×10^9 years prior to the collapse will have already supplied approximately 3×10^{10} erg/g, the energy per unit mass of the core after collapse would be 14.3×10^{10} erg/g, and this is just about twice the amount of energy shown by Ramsey to be needed for bringing about the phase-change. Evidently therefore the conditions are such that the collapse produces a superabundance of energy. The excess over that needed for the phase-change itself would further raise the temperature of the core-material. The energy would not of course be distributed in the same amount per unit mass everywhere within the core, since more work will be done on an element of mass at the centre, where the pressure is greatest, than on an element near the core-mantle boundary where the phase-change can necessarily only just be produced.

It has been seen how, after the collapse, the representative point for the Earth moves across to the thoroughly stable series Y'Q (Fig.6), along which further evolution will proceed steadily, with a time-scale of aeons, at a rate determined by the continuing increase of internal temperature. The evolution must still be occurring in order to bring about the decreasing moment-of-inertia implied by the ancient-eclipse data, and this requirement is fully in accord with the long half-lives of the radioactive elements that are the ultimate engine causing the evolution. Accompanying this is a decrease of the overall radius of the Earth (Tables 8 & 9) and thus of surface-area, and this feature is of the greatest importance where the formation of mountains is concerned. For about a century, geologists have been crying out for some specific process that would result in enormous amounts of contraction and compression of the outer layers of the Earth. Here is an example of such a plea from a well-known standard work on geology (Leet & Judson 1961) :

> One generalization on which all geologists agree is that mountain-building involves reduction in the surface-area of the globe - a shortening of the distance between points on the surface - and that all mountain-building is the product of a single mechanism - squeezing by horizontal compression. But when it comes to what causes the squeezing, there is no general agreement.

In regard to the final phrase, naturally enough there could be little hope of much agreement if the actual cause of the observed contraction had never been recognised. The only mildly serious explanation ever offered for it was the age-old thermal-contraction hypothesis, which to some extent could be examined theoretically in mathematical terms with a view to arriving at numerical estimates of its capabilities. However, even when all factors concerned were given what seemed optimal values for the success of the theory, the differential decrease in radius during the whole existence of an initially all-molten Earth through cooling, which was assumed to have been its course of evolution, could have amounted to no more than 10 km. But all along, geologists had maintained that this would provide quite an inadequate amount of contraction, while mainly failing to understand the over-riding objection that an initially all-molten state for the Earth is an inadmissible hypothesis anyway. Moreover, if thermal contraction were the cause of mountain-building, then on Mars, with its much lower surface-gravity into the bargain, there should also be folded and thrust mountains, whereas it is now known for certain, from the Mariner-photography of the whole surface, that there exist no signs of such features. (There are volcanic mountains, but these are not produced either on Earth or Mars by horizontal compressive forces, and so are not concerned here.) It has also long been known that such types of mountains have not been formed on the Moon, and in recent times the same has been established directly for the planet Mercury by photography of its surface during close flypasts.

It must be emphasised at the outset that, where mountain-building on the Earth is concerned, the real problem is not simply to account for the single most recent period, but to provide an explanation that will acount for possibly as many as twenty or more such eras of orogeny during the past history of the Earth. The phase-change theory leads to amounts of contraction quite adequate for this, as will be shown. Geologists have established that in the past 1500-million years there have occurred at least six major epochs of mountain building, four of them within the last 500-million years (Holmes 1965). As mentioned above, the immediate mechanism of mountain-formation has long been attributed to horizontal forces of compression, the direct consequences of which can be seen on every scale, but their ultimate source remained shrouded in obscurity. Where the deep interior is concerned, the pressures so greatly exceed the strength of materials that it will contract quite uniformly at all parts in response to the growth of the core through the gradual conversion of the innermost mantle-material to the core-phase, a process that must occur with perfect smoothness as the temperature rises in response to radioactive energy release. This however will not be so for the surface-layers, for in these the strength exceeds the pressure, and as their support from below is reduced, the outermost shell will become too large to fit the inner contracting volume and will be forced down by gravity, with the result that horizontal compressional stresses will automatically arise in it. At any places where these come to exceed the local strength, crumpling and thrusting of one layer over another will occur in order to reduce the effective (horizontally measured) area of contact with the underlying body of the Earth, and the outer-surface area will also undergo reduction, after the same manner as was claimed for thermal contraction.

The question might be asked, why a spherical shell of material at the surface should not simply stay there unaffected by contraction of the remainder of the Earth beneath it, just as an arched bridge is able to support itself against gravity. But it can readily be shown that the strength of the material is insufficient for this by orders of magnitude. For, consider a thin uniform spherical shell of density ρ, of outer radius a and inner radius b, unsupported from below but subject to radial gravity g. By symmetry, it will be under compressive stress everywhere in directions perpendicular to the radial direction. If now the shell is imagined to be cut through by a diametral plane, an average stress p, or force per unit area, would have to be applied round the perimeter to maintain equilibrium, as indicated in Fig. 11.

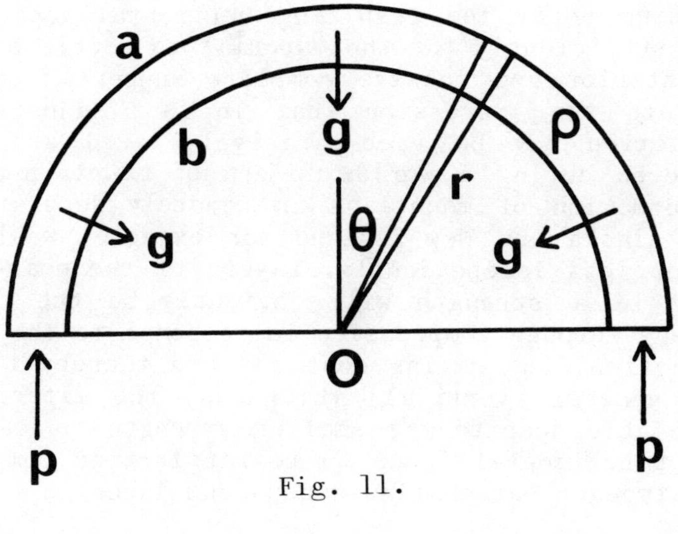

Fig. 11.

With the notation shown, the condition for equilibrium of the shell is

$$p.\pi(a^2 - b^2) = \int_b^a \int_0^{\pi/2} 2\pi r^2 \sin\theta \, d\theta \, dr. g\rho \cos\theta$$

$$= \frac{1}{3} \pi g\rho(a^3 - b^3). \qquad \ldots.(4)$$

If $a = R + \frac{1}{2}d$, $b = R - \frac{1}{2}d$, where d is small compared with R, this yields

$$p = \tfrac{1}{2} g\rho R(1 + d^2/12R^2) \qquad \ldots.(5)$$

With d of the order of 10-20 km, and R the radius of the Earth, the second term in d^2/R^2 is entirely negligible. Thus the average stress is practically independent of the depth of the layer, and given simply by the first term. For $g = 981$ cm/s^2, $\rho = 3.3$ g/cm^3 and $R = 6.37 \times 10^8$ cm, the requisite stress is $p = 1.03 \times 10^{12}$ dyn/cm^2. This exceeds the strength of any rocks by at least a factor 10^2, and thus even if support from below were reduced by only a few per cent, which could be allowed for in the calculation by adopting an effective gravity $g_e < g$, the material could not withstand the compressive forces, and the layers would adjust by folding and thrusting until the resulting horizontal area was reduced sufficiently for the material to settle back onto the interior and receive complete support from below. One gets the impression that in fact adjustments to contraction may be a comparatively local affair, and that even during a worldwide era of mountain-building the formation of mountains in remotely separated regions, Alaska and New Zealand for example, would occur more or less independently. Layers of the near-surface having least strength will obviously be the first to give way through compression in response to the general contraction, but having done so, and thereby increased their general (vertical) thickness, the material will become able despite the smaller strength to exert sufficient horizontal force to resist further compression by a stronger but shallower adjacent layer.

There can be no doubt that the most intense epoch of mountain-building of all will have occurred at the time of the initial collapse. The sudden decrease of outer radius by 70 km would have meant a reduction of circumference by about 440 km. Now granite, for example, can undergo compression lengthwise by about 1/800th before it fails, whereas in the collapse the circumference will be reduced by more than 1/100th. Thus if regarded as a continuous band of material, the outer layers could not resist compression after the radius had decreased by about 8 km, and in fact would probably fail in places much before this stage. Enforced decrease by nearly ten times this amount would obviously result in enormous amounts of folding and in extensive thrustings to reduce the surface-area. The total areal reduction (horizontally measured) that would have taken place is almost 12×10^6 km^2, rather more than 2 per cent of the whole original surface-area before collapse, and this could only be achieved by folding and thrusting on a prodigious scale. More impressive still than the surface-reduction is the total volume of material that would need somehow to be redisposed, and is almost 40×10^9 cubic-kilometres. But a proportion of this would consist of the lower-density molten material suddenly released below and welling up to the surface through linear fissures and vents created by fracture of its former solid constraining boundary, and so long as this material remained in molten form it would flow laterally and spread out over the surface. Seismic exploration of the present surface-layers has established that the continental material extends to considerable depths, in many places having thickness of nearly 70 km. Naturally enough, if this process is the explanation of continents, the depth would be expected to be greatest for the land-masses, as is found to be the case, but similar lighter material appears to extend to shallower depths of 10-20 km almost everywhere (Holmes 1965).

To proceed next to the course of evolution of the Earth after the collapse, it may be recalled first that the initial mass of the core would have been 0.3708×10^{27}g and its radius 2042 km, whereas the present values are 1.876×10^{27}g and 3477 km respectively (shown in

Table 8). The great differences in these figures give an indication of the immense range of evolution that must have occurred since the collapse. Where the surface radius is concerned, Table 8 shows that meanwhile it will have decreased from 6671.4 km (immediately after the collapse) to 6371.2 km at the present time, a reduction by almost exactly 300 km. If the collapse took place 3×10^9 years ago, this would mean an average rate of decrease of radius of no more than 0.01cm per year, far below anything susceptible of direct measurement even if it were occurring uniformly rather than intermittently. There can be nothing surprising about the average rate being as small as it is, for, were it to have been as large as, say, 0.1 cm per year, the Earth would have shrunk almost to nothing, besides which the resulting change of the moment-of-inertia would be occurring at far too great a rate to accord with the ancient-eclipse data.

In the following Table are shown the reduction of radius Δr_s, the reduction of (horizontally measured) surface-area ΔA, and the reduction in volume ΔV of the Earth as between the configuration immediately after collapse at time τ years ago and the present configuration, on the basis of G being constant. The differences for the several values of τ shown arise from the influence of radioactive heating on the value of the pressure p_{23} required to effect the phase-change at the interface between the outer-shell and mantle. A somewhat different empirical rule for p_{23} was adopted from that given by Eqn (4), Ch.7, p.140. The rule used in the calculations involved the assumed time of collapse, but the results showed that the properties of the 3-zone models were only minutely changed thereby.

TABLE 11

$\tau(10^9 yr)$	$\Delta r_S(km)$	$\Delta A(10^6 km^2)$	$\Delta V(10^9 km^3)$
-2.5	299	49.0	160
-3.0	294	48.2	157
-3.5	290	47.4	155
-4.0	285	46.4	152
-4.5	280	45.8	149

It is seen that for the larger values of τ the various changes are only slightly reduced in amount, and in particular the total volume of material to be redisposed at the surface is reduced over the whole range by less than ten per cent, which can in no way affect the general conclusions later drawn concerning the formation of mountains.

The present circumference of the Earth measures about 40,000 km, and if it were a continuous band of rock, a decrease by about 50 km would necessitate its yielding in some way. A 300-km decrease in radius, however, would mean a diminution of over 2000 km in the circumference, and thus on this simple basis a number of the order of 40 such relief-shortenings could be accounted for by this amount of contraction. This assumes the strength everywhere the same and equal to that of granite, and lesser strengths in places would increase the figure above 40. What would happen in practice is that stresses in the surface-layers (down to 20 km or so) would gradually build up until they began to exceed the strength, and then an era of mountain-building would commence, at the weakest places first, and then on to successive areas of greater strength until all stresses had been relieved, and the necessary reduction of surface-area achieved. Besides folding, thrustings of one layer over another would take place, or if already begun in previous eras would increase in their horizontal extent to help reduce the effective surface-area. Adjustment would be most intense to begin with and then gradually decay until a stage was reached when all stresses had been brought below the surface-strengths. The intervals between such periods of orogeny, if it is supposed that the round number of twenty have occurred in the history of the Earth, would be of order 1.5×10^8 years. It has been established from the geological record that the intervals separating major epochs of mountain-building are generally of this order.

Between these major epochs, contraction at the surface as a result of the continuing growth of the core would cease, pending the building-up of a fresh generation of surface-stresses. But with rising internal temperature, the level of phase-change corresponding to the 20°-discontinuity would progressively deepen. The mass of material in outer-shell form would therefore steadily increase at the expense of mantle-material, and the Earth would expand slightly, though on a scale far smaller than the contraction resulting from the growth of the core, and this expansion could well take the form of a slight rifting of the outer layers. Thus although over the whole history of the Earth to date, dr_s/dt would on average be strongly negative and equal to -300 km in 3 x 10^9 years, large decreases of radius, by as much as 10 - 20 km, would occur in the comparatively short periods of orogeny, while between them dr_s/dt could be numerically positive but small. Since the time of the Ramsey-collapse, say 3 x 10^9 years ago, p_{23} has probably increased owing to rise of temperature from about 0.09 x 10^{12} dyn/cm^2 to the present value of 0.14 x 10^{12} dyn/cm^2, and calculations show that through this effect (acting alone) the surface-radius r_s would increase by about 20 km. Accordingly in an interval of, say 1.5 x 10^8 years, between successive eras of mountain building, the radius would increase by just over 1 km, and the surface-area by about 1.7 x 10^5km^2. This figure is obviously not very sensitive in general order to the adopted initial value of p_{23}, and the resulting expansion of surface-area on any reasonable value would be rather greater than 10^5km^2 between successive eras. Clearly this increase could only be achieved by some kind of rifting at the tensionally weakest parts of the surface, and examples of such riftings are, in fact, known, though they are rare and occupy an area of the surface of the Earth minute compared with that covered by mountains. Thus the existence of such riftings is to be expected as a consequence of the Bernal phase-change now occurring at 413 km depth, but in no way tells against the far greater contraction of the Earth as a result of the mantle-core phase-change.

More impressive than the 2000-km reduction of circumference is the total surface-area that has somehow to be tucked away. The change of this is $\Delta(4\pi r_s^2)$, and for Δr_s = 300 km, this means total reduction by about 50 million square kilometres, about one-tenth the present surface-area of the globe. But the main physical change concerned is the volume of rock that has to be redisposed. No solid structure can extend above the general surface-level by more than 5 to 10 km : there cannot be terrestrial mountains 20 km high, because the floor below would have insufficient strength to support them, and if temporarily elevated to such height would proceed to sink down until the strength below could maintain them. The change of volume brought about by a decrease of radius by 300 km to the present value is no less than 160 billion cubic kilometres. Shared out for say 20 different eras of mountain building, this would mean $8 \times 10^9 km^3$ of rock to be redisposed somehow or other in each period. As an example of an idealized mountain-range, suppose its dimensions were 5 km high, 800 km in breadth, and 10,000 km in length (figures comparable with the dimensions of the Rocky Mountains), then its volume would be $4 \times 10^7 km^3$. Thus a volume of $8 \times 10^9 km^3$ would be able to provide for 200 such ranges in a single era of mountain building. This would certainly be adequate for the whole of the present mountains on Earth. It remains of course for geologists to decide whether these amounts of contraction that the phase-change theory inescapably leads to, and the implied rearrangement of material at the outer layers, are at last adequately comparable with those demanded by the facts.

Through weathering by climatic effects, of water, wind, and radiation, all mountains are being continually eroded with comparative rapidity. If no other process intervened, then in probably less than 10^8 years a complete erosion of the now-existing mountains and exposed land-surface would take place. The detritus would be carried as silt into the depths of the oceans and seas, and the whole surface of the Earth become covered with water to a depth of at least 2 - 3 km. Unless the mountains and ocean deeps were intermittently regenerated, the land-areas necessary for animal and plant-life of a non-marine nature would disappear altogether. But so long as the solar system, and the Earth in particular, undergoes no serious disturbance from unexpected astronomical causes, there is no reason to suppose that any such hostile environment will succeed the present distribution and proportion of land-masses, for the half-lives of uranium, thorium, and potassium are such that they will remain radioactive for aeons to come in sufficient abundance to continue to raise the internal temperature of the Earth and bring about further eras of mountain-building.

Finally, looking forward to the far-distant future, a time must come when the supply of energy from radioactivity in the interior must dwindle almost to nothing, and through continued escape of energy at the surface, the whole of the Earth will gradually cool down until it reaches the surface value of the temperature as maintained by external sources such as the Sun. In the course of this development, the phase-change process would now operate in the reverse direction. The level of the first phase-change, corresponding to the present 20°-discontinuity, will rise as a result of the lower pressure needed to effect it, and the Earth would thus contract slightly. But more important, core-material will revert to mantle-material as the temperature falls and be accompanied by expansion of the planet as a whole.

As far as mantle and core are concerned, the general evolution would now be in the reverse direction in the schematic diagram for a 2-zone planet, shown in Fig. 6, p.99. The representative-point would move along QY' through C until it reached X', at which stage it would jump rapidly to X, since evolution of the system could not take place along the unstable series. Physically this would mean that at first the liquid core would decrease gradually in mass, the planet meanwhile steadily expanding, but then immediately beyond X' the whole of the remainder of the core-material would be suddenly converted back to the mantle-phase accompanied by sudden expansion of the planet as a whole. Just as the initial Ramsey-collapse would be an implosion, so now this last stage would be an explosion of the planet. In view of the half-lives of the radioactive elements vitally concerned, the time taken to reach this final state of reversion to all-solid form might well be of order 10^{11} years, so far into the future that there could be small value in attempting to discuss the progress to it in any detail. Ramsey himself arrived in a general way at the possibility of an exploding planet and its relation to the time-honoured hypothesis for the origin of asteroids, but if it has to wait on the almost complete decay of these particular radioactive elements, it can scarcely be of relevance where production of presently existing members of the solar system are concerned.

REFERENCES AND NOTES

Holmes A. Principles of Physical Geology, Ronald, 1965.

Jeffreys H. Earthquakes and Mountains, Methuen, 1935.

Lees G.M. The Evolution of a Shrinking Earth. Quart.J. Geol.Soc. 109, 217, 1953.

The late Dr G.M.Lees, F.R.S., who spent his life in the field as a working geologist, was inflexible in his conclusion that at one time the Earth must have been far larger than at present, possibly by as much as 1,000 km in diameter ! The above reference is to his Presidential Address to the Geological Society of London in which he brings forward powerful geological arguments for his view.

Lyttleton R.A. On the Internal Structure of Mars, Mon. Not.Roy.Astron.Soc. 129, 21, 1965.

This paper showed that no folded or thrusted mountains would be found at the surface, but that rifting could be expected as a result of the Bernal phase-change, and also the absence of any dipole magnetic field. These predictions were subsequently verified in the Mariner-missions, but their implications for the theory of the structure of the Earth have gone unrecognised despite the fabulous cost of the missions.

Rutherford E. The Collected Papers of Lord Rutherford, Allen & Unwin, London, 1962.

It can scarcely have crossed the mind of Rutherford or any of his co-workers on radioactivity that their discoveries were of such relevance to the formation of mountains.

8

Application to the Other Terrestrial Planets

In accordance with the principle of uniformity in nature, the simplest assumption for the internal compositions of the terrestrial planets, Venus, Mars, Mercury, and of the Moon, is that they are similar to that of the Earth. On this basis, the seismic data for the Earth can be carried over directly and utilised for the calculation of the internal structure of these bodies. The equation of hydrostatic equilibrium shows that pressure always increases with depth, and it is a well-known result that the central pressure is least for a given gravitating mass if the density is everywhere uniform. The value is then given by

$$p_c \text{ (minimum)} = \frac{3GM^2}{8\pi R^4} , \qquad \ldots .(1)$$

where G is the constant of gravitation, and M and R the respective mass and radius of the planet. The following Table shows the values of the mass and radius, and the resulting minimum central-pressure for the five terrestrial bodies :

TABLE 12

	Mass (g)	Radius (km)	p_c(min)(dyn/cm^2)
Earth	5.976×10^{27}	6371	1.73×10^{12}
Venus	4.866×10^{27}	6055	1.40×10^{12}
Mars	6.434×10^{26}	3394	2.48×10^{11}
Mercury	3.313×10^{26}?	2443?	2.45×10^{11}
Moon	7.350×10^{25}	1738	4.72×10^{10}

Allowance for compressibility always has the effect of decreasing the radius and increasing the central pressure, and therefore, since p_c(min) for Venus is already greater than the pressure at the mantle-core boundary in the Earth (1.37×10^{12} dyn/cm^2), it follows that Venus will also have three main zones. On the other hand, the minimum central pressures in Mars and Mercury are almost a factor of 10 less than the pressure at the core-mantle boundary in the Earth, and calculations show that allowance for compression falls far short of bringing the central pressure up to this value. Accordingly Mars and Mercury, on the present basis, would be 2-zone all-solid planets, with no phase-change liquid core, but as will be seen later, if the presently current values of the mass and radius of Mercury (queried above) are correct, this planet must have significantly different composition from other members of the terrestrial group. Where the Moon is concerned, p_c(min) is only about one-third of that prevailing at the 20°-discontinuity level in the Earth where it is reached at a depth of a mere 150 km. Allowance for compression increases from this minimum of 4.72×10^{10}dyn/cm^2 only to 4.80×10^{10}dyn/cm^2, and the Moon must therefore be a 1-zone body with no phase-change discontinuities anywhere in it of the kind occurring in the Earth at 413-km depth and 2898-km depth. We now take the several bodies in turn and consider their internal structures.

VENUS

Until recent years with the advent of radar techniques, there was little possibility of determining the radius of the solid-surface of Venus with any worthwhile accuracy because of the presence of a deep atmosphere of uncertain detailed composition and impenetrable at optical wavelengths. But even at that stage, both the mass and radius were sufficiently close to those of the Earth to suggest that the two planets might be expected to have similar internal structures. Even if the radius of about 6150 km to the visible cloud-surface were adopted for the solid radius, then with the same physical properties as those of the Earth, calculations show that Venus must possess a central liquid core, for any all-solid model of Venus has a radius in excess of 6250 km. But the atmosphere is not opaque to radar-wavelengths, and measures of the radius of the solid-surface, from which such waves are reflected, have in recent years been achieved with almost kilometric accuracy. Numerous independent measures have been made, and the net results of these combine to give a mean-radius somewhere between 6050 and 6060 km. For present purposes, adoption of the median value of 6055 km is of ample accuracy. This means that Venus has radius about 0.95 of the Earth. For the mass of Venus, M_V, flypasts by spacecraft have refined the mass-value to the numerical value shown in the above Table of 4.866×10^{27}g, or about 0.814 of the mass of the Earth.

If the pressure p_{12} at the core-mantle interface were known for Venus, and also the pressure p_{23} for the phase-change from mantle to outer-shell material, then a unique model could be calculated, and would lead to a theorteical surface-radius. On the other hand, if the outer radius r_S is assigned, it would be necessary for only one of the pressures p_{12} and p_{23} to be fixed in order to arrive at a unique model. Since little is yet understood in more than a qualitative way of how pressure and temperature affect the core-mantle phase-change, it is preferable to consider how the value of p_{23} may be suitably assigned. In the Earth, p_{23} is known to be 0.141×10^{12}dyn/cm^2, a pressure that can nowadays be readily obtained in laboratory-experiments, which have shown that this phase-change is quite sensitive to temperature, higher pressure being required to produce it at higher temperature of the material. As will be seen later, the internal structure of Mars is in accord with this.

Where the internal temperature of Venus is concerned, on the present basis the general distribution through radioactive heating would be much the same as for the Earth, other things being equal, but its closer proximity to the Sun could mean higher temperature of the material from which it originally formed. Moreover, at the surface of Venus the temperature maintained by solar heating is about 750K as compared with 300K for the Earth. Taken together, these considerations indicate that p_{23} will be somewhat greater in Venus than in the Earth. The following Table shows, for the adopted values 6050 kms and 6060 kms of the radius, the values of the core-mass m_C, its proportion of the whole mass m_V, and the pressure p_{12} at the core-mantle boundary corresponding to assigned values of

$$p_{23} = 0.016 \times 10^{12} \text{ dyn/cm}^2$$

$$p_{23} = 0.15 \times 10^{12} \text{ dyn/cm}^2$$

$$p_{23} = 0.14 \times 10^{12} \text{ dyn/cm}^2$$

for 3-zone models of Venus.

TABLE 13

	p_{23} (10^{12} dyn/cm^2) assigned =	0.16	0.15	0.14
r_S = 6050 km	m_c (10^{27} g)	1.226	1.209	1.190
	m_c/M_V	0.252	0.249	0.245
	p_{12} (10^{12} cgs)	1.224	1.229	1.234
r_S = 6060 km	m_c (10^{27} g)	1.184	1.167	1.148
	m_c/M_V	0.243	0.240	0.236
	p_{12} (10^{12} cgs)	1.234	1.239	1.244

These values of p_{12} range from 1.224 - 1.244 x 10^{12}dyn/cm^2, but all are seen to be less than the corresponding pressure in the Earth of 1.37 x 10^{12}dyn/cm^2. If we take the phase-change hypothesis, we find the results suggest that the central regions of Venus are at <u>higher</u> temperature than the corresponding parts of the Earth, for the mantle-core phase-change is such that at higher temperature it can be produced by lower pressure. Calculations show that <u>if</u> the core-boundary pressure p_{12} in Venus were taken equal to the terrestrial value of 1.37 x 10^{12} dyn/cm^2, the resulting radius r_S for any reasonable value of p_{23} would be about 6200 km, which is obviously inadmissibly too large. Thus there can be little doubt that p_{12} for Venus <u>must</u> be lower than in the Earth at present.

The mass in the core is seen from Table 13 to be at most 25.2 per cent of M_V compared with 31.4 per cent for the Earth. On the phase-change theory, with the composition the same throughout and the same for both planets, the difference results chiefly from the smaller mass (0.814 M_E), and to some extent from the higher internal temperature. On the iron-core hypothesis, it would imply a serious difference in relative compositions of the two planets, and this in turn would need special explanation. If Venus possessed a liquid core with 31.4 of the whole mass, which uniformity would require on the iron-core notion, calculations show that with any acceptable value of p_{23}, the outer solid-radius could not be greater than about 5980 km, some 70 km less than any radar-determination, and again a quite inadmissible value.

The proportionate difference, as between the Earth and Venus, of their core-mantle interface-pressures is seen from the above Table to be about 0.1, and if the corresponding differences of internal temperatures $\Delta T/T$ at corresponding levels is of the same order as $\Delta p_{12}/p_{12}$ but of opposite sign, this would mean a temperature distribution in Venus systematically higher by a few hundred degrees, and such a difference is definitely established for the present surface-conditions. From all these considerations, it emerges that probably the most satisfactory present model for Venus is that

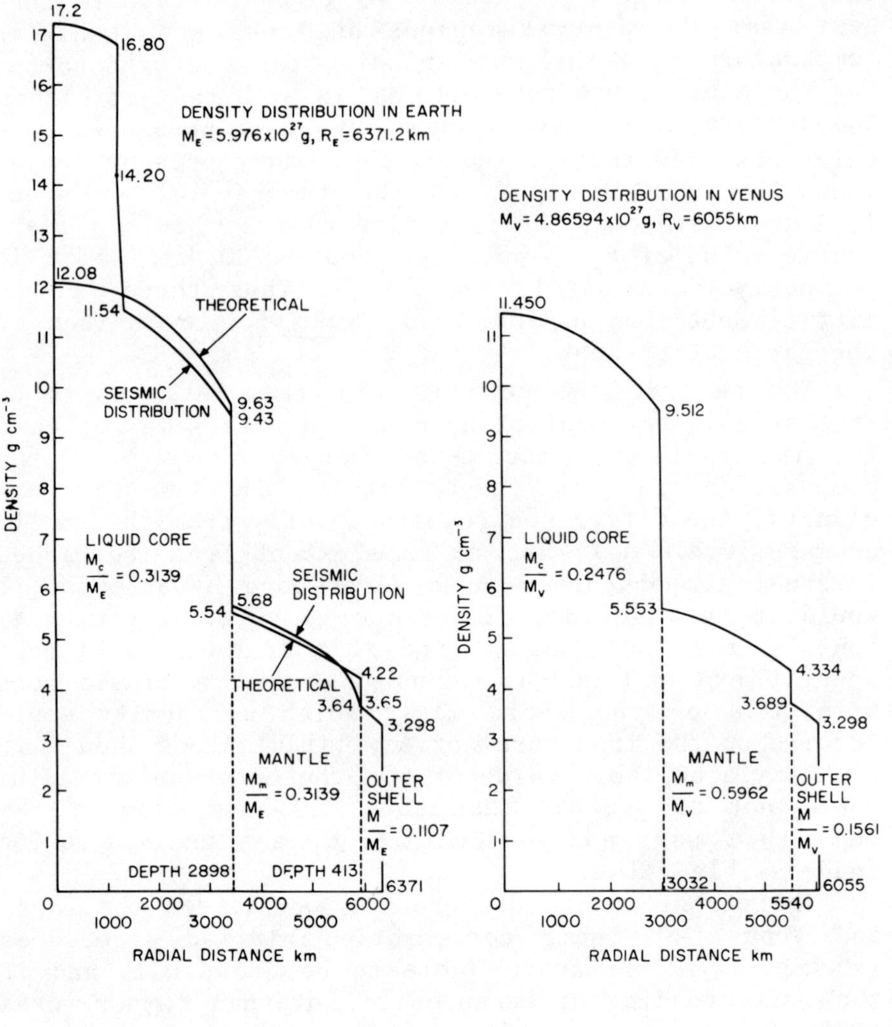

Fig. 12
Comparison of the theoretical density distribution of Venus with that of the Earth. (The seismic distribution also shown for the Earth has been drawn from values given by Bullen.)

calculated for the values r_s = 6055 km, and p_{12}= 0.16 x 10^{12} dyn/cm^2 (See Fig. 12). The main results satisfying these conditions for a 3-zone model are as follows :

TABLE 14

Three-zone Model of Venus

Mass of Venus $M_V = 4.866 \times 10^{27}$ g

Surface-radius $r_s = 6055 \times 10^5$ cm

$m_c = 1.205 \times 10^{27}$ g $= 0.248\ M_V$

$\rho_c = 11.45$ g/cm^3

$p_c = 2.702 \times 10^{12}$dyn/cm^2

$r_c = 3032$ km $= 0.501\ r_s$

$p_{12} = 1.229 \times 10^{12}$dyn/cm^2

$r_m = 5540$ km $= 0.915\ r_s$

$m_{12} = 4.106 \times 10^{27}$g $= 0.844\ M_V$

$p_{23} = 0.16 \times 10^{12}$cgs (assigned)

$\rho_m = 5.233$ g/cm^3

$f = 0.3424$ (moment-of-inertia factor)

$-W = 0.1703 \times 10^{40}$ erg

$g_s = 885.0$ cm/s^2 (surface-gravity)

In the same way as for the Earth, we may also calculate how large Venus would be, together with other properties, before the planet reached the stage of core formation : that is, the size of an all-solid 2-zone model for Venus. With the same notation as for the Earth, the values found are as follows :

TABLE 15 All-solid two-zone model of Venus

m_c = 4.296×10^{27} g = 0.883 M_V

ρ_c = 5.708 g/cm^3

p_c = 1.41583×10^{12} cgs

r_c = 5954 km = 0.944 r_s (all-solid)

p_{12} = p_{23} = 0.098×10^{12} cgs

r_s = 6306 km

f = 0.3776

-W = 0.1547×10^{40} erg

Here the core-mass m_c is the total mass of material in mantle-form before the phase-change giving a liquid core commences. The value of $p_{12} = p_{23}$ is chosen to accord with the earlier discussion to the effect that this phase-change will have required lower pressure to produce it in the initial stages of the planet with its internal temperatures lower, but the results are not importantly affected if some slightly different value is adopted. It is seen that the surface-radius of 6306 km is some 251 km greater than the present value. Thus Venus will have evolved and contracted in a similar manner to the Earth, but the proportionate decrease of overall radius is markedly less for Venus, and thus a smaller proportion of the mass can be expected to be in the form of a phase-changed liquid core, as Table 14 shows to be the case.

When a series of 3-zone models of Venus for increasing values of the core-mass as parameter are calculated, the same phenomenon is found as for the Earth, namely that the pressure p_{12} at the boundary between core and mantle at first increases above the original central value of 1.416×10^{12}dyn/cm^2 for the all-solid 2-zone model. The actual figures are as in the following Table, with p_{12} given to 5 decimal places the better to illustrate the effect :

TABLE 16

$m_c (10^{27} g)$	$p_c (10^{12} cgs)$	$\rho_c (g\ cm^{-3})$	$p_{12} (10^{12} cgs)$	$r_c (km)$	$r_s (km)$	$-W (10^{40} erg)$
0.0		(5.708)				
+0.0	1.45183	9.815	1.41583	+ 0.0	6306.2	.15466
0.04	1.560	10.03	1.42502	987.7	6298.3	.15520
0.06	1.604	10.10	1.42575	1129.6	6294.3	.15546
0.07	1.624	10.13	(max)1.42583	1188.7	6292.3	.15560
0.08	1.642	10.15	1.42577	1242.4	6290.4	.15573
0.12	1.711	10.25	1.42443	1420.3	6282.4	.15627
0.16	1.772	10.33	1.42187	1561.6	6274.4	.15680
0.20	1.827	10.41	1.41843	1680.7	6266.4	.15734
0.22604	1.8608	10.46	1.41583	1749.7	6261.1	.15769

The two values for the central density shown for $m_c = 0$ correspond to an all-solid 2-zone model therefore with no liquid core, and to a 3-zone model with liquid core of mass $m_c = +\ 0.0$ infinitesimally greater than zero. Their ratio is $\lambda = 1.72$, and hence indicates that the Ramsey-collapse will have occurred for Venus.

As in the Table of 3-zone Earth-models (Table 8, p.119) it is seen that the core-mantle interface pressure p_{12} at first <u>increases</u> steadily with m_c to a maximum of about 1.42583×10^{12} dyn/cm^2 for m_c very close to 0.07×10^{27}g, and then decreases steadily to attain the original value $p_c(m_c = 0)$ of 1.41583×10^{12}dyn/cm^2 which it reaches when $m_c = 0.22604 \times 10^{27}$g, which is slightly over 4.6 per cent of the whole mass. This rise and fall of p_{12}, as explained for the Earth, is the way that the Ramsey-collapse manifests itself when the 3-zone series is followed by stationary models. The initial size of the core is seen to be 1749.7 km, and thus is a 'large core' in the Ramsey sense, while the outer-radius immediately after collapse is 6261.1 km. The sudden decrease in surface-radius is by 45 km, compared with 70 km in the collapse of the Earth. The resulting reduction of surface-area is by 7.12×10^6 km^2, while the reduction in total volume of the planet is by 22.4×10^9 km^3. These sudden decreases would be more than sufficient to provide for an immediate first era of mountain-building on a global scale. (The present surface-area of Venus is 461×10^6 km^2.) The subsequent evolution after collapse, as a result of continued radioactive heating, would follow the same general course as for the Earth : the core-mass and its radius now steadily increasing, with the planet thoroughly stable at all stages, and the overall (theoretical) surface-radius steadily decreasing.

It is seen from Table 14 that the present liquid-core radius in Venus is 3032 km, and so has increased by 1282 km since the collapse, while the proportion of mass in the core has increased from 4.65 per cent to 24.8 per cent of the total mass. Accompanying this evolution, the outer radius <u>decreases</u> by 206 km over and above the initial sudden decrease by 45 km. The present depth of the first phase-change (corresponding to the 20°-discontinuity in the Earth) amounts to $r_s - r_m$ = 515 km, as compared with 413 km in the Earth. The total release of gravitational energy in the evolution from the all-solid stage to the present one is seen from Tables 14 and 15 to be 1.56 x 10^{38} erg, or 3.21 x 10^{10} erg per gram for the entire planet, though as in the case of the Earth, somewhat more than 70 per cent of this energy goes to doing work on the core-material, and most of the remainder to the work needed to compress the solid mantle during the gradual collapse. These values may be compared with the corresponding figures for the Earth of 2.88 x 10^{38} erg, and 4.81 x 10^{10} erg/g.

Where mountain-building is concerned, the total decrease of radius of Venus has been from 6306 km when in all-solid form to the present value of 6055 km. The accompanying decrease of surface-area is about 40 x 10^6 square kilometres, while the reduction in total volume is 120 x 10^9 cubic kilometres, the corresponding amounts for the Earth having been seen to be 50 x 10^6 km^2, and 160 x 10^9 km^3 (Table 11, p.142). Thus, it follows that folded and thrusted mountains can be expected to have formed on Venus to an extent approaching that on Earth. Indeed, since the central pressure when in all-solid form, i.e. 1.416 x 10^{12} dyn/cm^2 is substantially less than that in the Earth when in all-solid form, 1.634 x 10^{12} dyn/cm^2, considerably higher temperature would be needed in the central region of Venus to bring about conditions for the phase-change. Thus Venus may have remained all-solid for a time of perhaps a billion years longer than did the Earth, and there would be an equal reduction of the time since mountain-building commenced. But once started, the intervals between successive major eras of orogeny may have been much the same as for the Earth.

That there would be mountains of folded and thrusted types on Venus was an inevitable prediction once the phase-change theory had been developed for the structure of the Earth. It was first made in the early 1960s before the introduction of the radar-techniques by which alone it could be directly verified. The first success of their application to Venus was to establish the sidereal rotation-period of the planet, which had long been known to be incapable of precise measurement by optical means. The unexpected result emerged that the rotation is <u>retrograde</u> with a period of 242.98 days. Large-scale surface-irregularities were also detected by Earth-based measures, and the regular return of these areas of Venus to presentation towards the Earth has enabled the period to be determined with high accuracy. It was an obvious possibility that these large-scale irregularities were some form of mountains, and recent topographical mappings by surface-imaging from the Pioneer-Venus orbiting satellite have identified some of these features as having elevations of 5 to 10 km above the surrounding terrain, together with numerous other signs of tectonic activity.

A contour-map of an area now referred to as the Beta-Complex shows differences of some 8 km over horizontal distances of about 1000 km, while another area covering the strange Maxwell-feature and a great plateau shows differences of heights of 10 km over distances of only 800 km. These are some of the preliminary results, but the indications are strong that the surface layers of Venus are as active and irregular as those of the Earth. If folded and thrusted mountains are in fact present on Venus, it is an open question to what extent they will resemble terrestrial mountains, the general appearance of which is much the result of rainfall and erosion producing canyons, and smaller canyons within these, and so on, for example. The atmosphere of Venus is almost two orders of magnitude greater in mass than that of the Earth, and it is now known to consist principally of carbon-dioxide : the surface-pressure is 94 terrestrial atmospheres at a density of 0.065 g/cm^3 (fifty times air-density at ground-level) and the surface-temperature 768K. Conditions are therefore likely to be very different from those at the surface of the Earth, but it is not known to what extent, if any, precipitation onto the surface occurs, corresponding to rainfall on Earth, that could bring about erosion and weathering. A project termed VOIR (Venus Orbiting Imaging Radar), planned for a few years hence, aims at achieving highly detailed mapping of the whole surface, and should make it easily possible to see if any features resembling the Rockies, Andes, or Himalayas exist at the surface.

If Venus has any dipole magnetic field, it is so small that as yet it has escaped measurement, which places the magnetic moment at no more than 0.0001 that of the Earth. The origin of the terrestrial magnetic field is by no means well understood, though it seems certain that it is generated in some way by electric currents in the liquid-core. As far as the phase-change hypothesis is concerned, the liquid-metallic phase of the core-material is equally as suitable as molten iron for the purpose. The Earth is a rapidly spinning body (compared with its orbital rate), and it is possible that the lunar and solar couples, which enforce its precession, are the ultimate sources of the energy needed to maintain the currents. Venus, however, as has been seen, rotates extremely slowly by comparison with the Earth, while just because of this slow rotation any sensible differences of moments of inertia can result only from topographical features and local density differences, and must be far smaller than for the Earth. Thus the planet may have three slightly different principal moments of inertia and not undergo any steady precession, as do rapidly rotating planets such as the Earth or Mars, which have two principal moments of inertia almost equal. In the absence of any reliable theory of the generation of the magnetic field, it is only possible to speculate that it may depend directly on ω, the rate of rotation of the planet, or even on ω^2, in which case it would be understandable that for Venus it would be far less than for the Earth.

MARS

Table 12, p.150 shows that the central pressure in Mars must exceed about 0.248×10^{12} dyn/cm^2, and calculations show that compression increases this only to just over 0.28×10^{12} dyn/cm^2, a pressure that occurs in the Earth high up in the solid mantle at a depth of only about 750 km. Since the radius of Mars is only little more than half that of the Earth, radioactive heating would be likely to produce a generally lower internal temperature-distribution, since escape of energy at the surface mass-for-mass would be greater, while at the distance of Mars from the Sun the material originally going to form the planet would be substantially cooler than at the distance of the Earth, and any heating by adiabatic compression would be less, mass-for-mass, than in the Earth. Certainly the planet could not have been at higher temperature in its deep interior than the Earth at any stage. Accordingly this far lower central pressure means that there is no possibility of conditions within Mars ever having become suitable for the phase-change to the terrestrial-core state, and on the present basis the planet would be effectively all solid. Since the 20°-discontinuity occurs in the Earth at a pressure of 0.14×10^{12}dyn/cm^2 this phase-change must certainly also occur in Mars, and the planet consist of two main zones, an inner zone with properties the same as the terrestrial mantle and an outer zone with properties the same as the outer-shell of the Earth. Also, in view of the likelihood of a lower internal temperature in Mars, this phase-change may be expected to occur at lower pressure than in the Earth, and this is borne out by calculations, as may be seen from Table 17.

Just as for all-solid models of the Earth and Venus, calculations can be made of two-zone models of Mars for a series of values of the core-mass m_c, now having the properties of terrestrial mantle-material. The following Table 17 shows results covering a range of the interface-pressure from $(0.1356 - 0.0473) \times 10^{12}$dyn/cm^2. It is seen, by interpolation, that a model for which $m_c = 0.4119 \times 10^{27}$g would have surface-radius equal to the observed value of 3394 km, and that the corresponding interface pressure is 0.068×10^{12} dyn/cm^2. This is in accord with the planet having lower internal temperature distribution than the Earth. The depth at which the transition occurs is 560 km, compared with 413 km in the Earth, but this is to be accounted for by the much weaker gravity, which at the surface of Mars has value 372 cm/s^2 compared with 981 cm/s^2 for the Earth.

If the view is correct that the main magnetic field of the Earth arises from forced motions within its

TABLE 17

m_c (10^{27}g)	ρ_c (g cm^{-3})	p_c (10^{12}cgs)	r_c (km)	p_{int} (10^{12}cgs)	r_s (km)	f	$-W$ (10^{38}erg)	ρ_m (g cm^{-3})
0.2	4.502	.2697	2217.6	.1356	3463.5	.38209	.48951	3.697
0.3	4.513	.2778	2543.9	.1024	3431.7	.38032	.49513	3.800
0.4	4.521	.2831	2806.0	.0713	3398.1	.38104	.49947	3.914
0.42	4.522	.2840	2853.3	.0652	3391.2	.38149	.50017	3.938
0.44	4.523	.2847	2899.2	.0592	3384.1	.38206	.50083	3.963
0.46	4.524	.2854	2943.8	.0533	3376.9	.38275	.50142	3.988
0.48	4.525	.2859	2987.2	.0473	3369.7	.38355	.50196	4.014

liquid core in response to the precession of the containing rigid mantle, it would follow that no main dipole field of internal origin can exist on Mars, even though its obliquity and rotation-period are both very nearly the same as for the Earth, while its precession rate is not negligible at about one-seventh that of the Earth. This clear-cut prediction was made on the basis of the phase-change theory considerably before it was directly verified during the Mariner-IV fly-past of Mars in July 1965. No dipole-field was detected by the magnetometer carried on the craft, and the sensitivity of the instrument implied that if any such field were present it must have magnetic-moment less than 1/3000 that of the Earth. Of course an extremely small induced field resulting from the interaction of the solar-wind with the planet and its ionosphere is not ruled out. The argument can now be reversed, and from the absence of any measurable field can be inferred the absence of any sizable metallic core in the planet.

If Mars has similar composition to the Earth, including radioactive content of the interior, it will have begun its existence as an individual planet with a systematically lower internal temperature distribution than at present, and thus the initial interface-pressure would have been even lower than now. As seen from the above Table 17, this would mean that the planet would have had smaller overall radius, and an increase of p_{12} by as little as 0.01×10^{12} dyn/cm^2 will be accompanied by an increase of r_S by about 12km. This in turn would imply an increase of (horizontally measured) surface-area of just over 10^6 km^2 (the present total surface-area being about 144×10^6 km^2), and proportionally greater for a larger increase of p_{12}. It should be noted that such an expansion of the planet is not ordinary thermal expansion, but results from material in the denser crystal-phase changing back to the less-dense packing as temperature rises, and therefore occupying greater volume. Clearly this will take place at and near the interface, but the surface-layers will adjust to the change going on deep below by rifting to relieve the tensile stresses that would be steadily built up in them, and further rise in temperature could be accommodated by already existing rifts broadening still further. Thermal expansion, on the other hand, merely increases the volume everywhere without producing stresses. Thus areas of the Martian surface would be expected to be covered by deep channels or trenches. Here again, this was predicted before any spacecraft flew to Mars, on the basis of the Bernal phase-change in the Earth, and the subsequent detailed photography has disclosed numerous such rifts at many parts of the surface, the most extensive example of which is the now famed Valles Marineris with its prodigious dimensions compared with any terrestrial canyons.

On the other hand, since the central pressure is far too low for the change to metallic-liquid form, there can be no possibility of Mars ever having undergone contraction, and the phase-change theory enabled it to be predicted that there would be no folded and thrusted mountains found on the planet. Volcanic mountains are not ruled out, of course, for these do not result from horizontal forces of compression ; indeed, the great Mons Olympus rises some 25 km above the general surface of Mars. If on the principle of uniformity an iron core existed in Mars carrying just over 31 per cent of the total mass, then even with p_{12} as high as 0.14×10^{12} dyn/cm^2 (the value in the Earth) the theoretical radius is found to fall short of the observed value by about 150 km. Only if the planet contains a negligible or no iron core can the calculated radius be made to agree with the actual value.

The present values of the mass and radius of Mars are entirely consistent with the planet being of two main zones constituted of material with the same physical properties as the mantle and outer-shell of the Earth. In addition to this consistency, the phase-change theory requires that there should be no dipole magnetic field, and also that there should be no folded and thrusted mountain-systems such as are so widespread on the Earth. Moreover, the known factors associated with the 20°-discontinuity in the Earth, when applied to Mars, adequately account for the observed sunderings and riftings at the surface.

THE MOON

The theoretical structure of the Moon, regarded as a small terrestrial planet, is also entirely consistent with the present basis. There emerges no reason to suppose it to have essentially different composition from the outer-shell of the Earth, though the extreme outer-layers of a few kilometres depth, shielded by no atmosphere of note, have been subjected to bombardment from without by particles as small as atoms at one extreme to gigantic meteorites capable of forming seas or maria at the other. The mathematical theory of planetary structure cannot encompass the peculiarities of the near-surface structure, any more than the theory of stellar structure accounts for the sunspot phenomenon. Even more so than with Mars, there can be no mountains of folded or thrusted type on the Moon because of its small mass of only about one-tenth that of Mars. There are features on the surface which for the sake of a name are called 'mountains', just as the word 'seas' is a misnomer, but the former can be recognised to be the eroded rims of some of the oldest large craters.

The Moon has mass 0.0735×10^{27}g and radius of about 1738 km, and the central pressure can only slightly exceed that for a uniform sphere of these dimensions. This minimum pressure of 0.0472×10^{12}dyn/cm^2 is attained in the Earth at a depth of only about 150 km, and therefore the phase-change corresponding to the 20°-discontinuity in the Earth cannot be expected to occur in the Moon. It will thus be a one-zone body composed of material having the same elastic properties and uncompressed density as the outer-shell of the Earth, and calculations based on these together with the mass (but with no assumption as to the radius) yield the following results :

TABLE 18

One-zone Model of the Moon

ρ_c	= 3.427 g/cm^3	f	= 0.39823
p_c	= 0.04802 x 10^{12} cgs	ρ_m	= 3.350 g/cm^3
r_s	= 1736.93 km	g_s	= 162.5 cm/s^2

According to recent direct determinations, the mean surface-radius of the Moon is 1737.63 ± 0.11 km. and the theoretically calculated radius is thus only 0.70 km less than this. A defect in this direction is not surprising, for, as a result of the weak lunar-gravity field, only at depths exceeding about 20 km would the hydrostatic pressure dominate over the strength of the material, and the distribution at lesser depths would not be one of strictly hydrostatic equilibrium. Any naturally arising departure from this would automatically involve less compression and so give a slightly larger radius. Then again there is the possibility of a shallow surface-layer of dust and rubble with effective volume-density lower than the standard uncompressed density of the material. The existence of such a layer would also have the effect of reducing the moment-of-inertia factor f slightly, and an increase so produced in the observed radius could result in a decrease of f by about 0.0003.

The value of f differs so little from that for a uniform sphere, 0.4, as to imply that the Moon is only slightly compressed throughout its whole volume. If free from any compression, the Moon would have radius 1745.99 km, only 8.36 km greater than the observed value, and 9.06 km greater than the theoretical value. That there can be only a slight degree of concentration of mass towards the centre is also shown by the small amounts by which the central density exceeds both the mean density and the uncompressed density. The conclusion is quite inescapable that the Moon cannot contain any substantial proportion of free iron, either in the form of a central core, or elsewhere. If 31.4 per cent of its mass resided in an iron core, the proportion claimed for the Earth on the iron-core hypothesis, the overall radius would be less than 1450 km, nearly 300 km short of the observed value. Thus on the iron-core theory, it would be necessary to explain how the Moon, presumably forming in close proximity to the Earth in the original solar nebula, either as a satellite almost from the outset or as a close-by independent planet later to be captured, came to receive no more than a negligible amount of free iron. On the phase-change theory, there is clearly no anomaly to be explained.

MERCURY

Mercury appears to be an especially interesting planet from a cosmogonical standpoint, for it happens to be the one member of the terrestrial group, on present determinations of its mass and radius, which fails to conform to the principle of uniformity of composition which is satisfied by the other terrestrial planets and the Moon. Because of its extremely small mass and its proximity to the Sun, both the mass and radius have always presented difficulty of accurate determination, and the mean-density, depending as it does on the inverse cube of its radius, even more so. In 1947, a review of planetary structures by Wildt gave the mass and radius as

$$M = 0.2028 \times 10^{27}\text{g}, \quad r_s = 2530 \text{ km}, \qquad \ldots.(2)$$

implying a mean-density of only 2.86 g/cm^3, less than that of the Moon. A new determination of the mass by Rabe (1950) from the perturbations of Eros, depending on earlier work by Stracke (1940), led to a value of the mass greater by a factor of about 1.6, while the optically determined radius was considered to be slightly less. This was prior to the application of radar-techniques to the problem, and the revised values then current were

$$M = 0.323 \times 10^{27}\text{g}, \quad r_s = 2495 \pm 125 \text{ km} \quad \ldots.(3)$$

which yield $\rho_m = 4.96\ g/cm^3$.

This value of the mass was based on observations of the minor planet Eros over several decades, and for many years was regarded as a more accurate value than any hitherto obtained from the perturbations in the longitude of Venus, which when expressed in the standard form of periodic terms have coefficients such that the greatest produced by Mercury is rather less than 0".4, an angle smaller than the accuracy with which individual measures can be made of (the centre of the disc of) Venus itself. But the whole investigation was later found by Rabe himself (1967) to be vitiated by a serious conceptual error, and upon this being rectified, the mass of Mercury, as derived from observations of Eros, turned out to be almost completely indeterminate, the probable error being comparable with the (reciprocal) mass itself.

However, the most recent announcement of the mass, following the Mariner Venus-Mercury flypasts is not very different from that of (3) curiously enough, while the corresponding value of the radius is given as somewhat less and with much smaller error-ranges. These values are

$$M = 0.3313 \pm 0.0018 \times 10^{27} g, \qquad r_s = 2442.8 \pm 0.5\ km \qquad ....(4)$$

corresponding to a mean-density of $5.43\ g/cm^3$, almost as high as that of the Earth.

Even with these latest values for the mass and radius, there is no possibility of the central pressure in Mercury being anywhere near that required for the phase-change to the metallic liquid form to give a terrestrial type core. As for the values themselves, they can readily be fitted by a 2-zone model consisting of an iron-core surrounded by material with properties the same as those of the outer-shell of the Earth, the pressure at the base of which turns out to be considerably less than the value $0.14 \times 10^{27} dyn/cm^2$ at the 20°-discontinuity in the Earth. The ad-hoc adoption of iron for the composition of the core would be by no means essential, and any other substance with high uncompressed density would lead to a consistent model (as for example, mercury itself if a metallic liquid core is regarded as of special appeal !). But as iron has long been preferred, it would be a departure from tradition to postulate anything else at this stage.

The point of cosmogonical interest is to determine what proportion of the mass would need to be in the form of free iron in a central core to satisfy these latest values of the mass and radius. For this purpose, a linear law of the usual form $k = a + 3.5p$ can be adopted for the bulk-modulus of iron. As some slight uncertainty may attach to the value of $\underline{a}$ under conditions prevailing within Mercury (as compared with laboratory-conditions), calculations have been made for the three values (1.5, 1.6, 1.7) x 10^{12}dyn/cm^2, and from these it emerges that the resulting proportion of iron depends only weakly on the value of $\underline{a}$. For the mass and radius, the numerical values adopted were 0.330 x 10^{27}g and 2440 km respectively, the calculations having been made prior to the latest values (4) being announced, but the small differences cannot importantly affect the numerical results, which are shown in the following Table :

TABLE 19

Two-zone Iron-core Models of Mercury

	$a=1.5 \times 10^{12}$	$a=1.6 \times 10^{12}$	$a=1.7 \times 10^{12}$
ρ_c(g/cm^3)	9.619	9.518	9.427
p_c(10^{12}cgs)	0.4483	0.4441	0.4403
m_c(10^{27}g)	0.2000	0.2009	0.2016
m_c/M	0.6061	0.6068	0.6109
r_c(km)	1755	1761	1767
p_{int}(10^{12}cgs)	0.0918	0.0908	0.0899
f	0.3252	0.3258	0.3264
-W(10^{38}erg)	0.1993	0.1991	0.1988

It is seen that an iron-core carrying rather more than 60 per cent of the entire mass is demanded by the data for any of the three values of _a_. Also, the central pressures are much too small for any mantle-core phase-change, while the pressures at the interface are far smaller still. Three-zone models of Mercury have also been calculated consisting of an iron-core, surrounded by mantle-type material, and then an outer-shell. The percentage of mass required in the iron-core is found to be reduced slightly to just under 60 per cent, so the general conclusion is not altered. Since iron and rocky materials are the substances in contention for the compositions of other members of the terrestrial group, and if only these are considered, it may be concluded on present results that Mercury has a highly unusual constitution. Attempts have been made to account for this by associating it with the proximity of Mercury to the Sun, but the temperatures that would be maintained at the orbital distance of Mercury are not such as would come anywhere near melting iron or rock, never mind vaporising them, to permit of differentiation, and there is no reason to suppose that such temperatures could in any way bring about so striking a disparity. Moreover, if any such effect were operative, it would seem probable that it would also manifest itself, at least to some extent, in the composition of Venus. But as has been seen, the internal structure of Venus presents no suggestion of any similar anomaly, and is satisfactorily calculable on the hypothesis that it is similarly constituted to the Earth.

Curiously enough the physical properties and the appearance of the surface of Mercury closely resemble those of the Moon, and give no hint of any underlying excess of iron. As the internal pressures on any basis are far too low for the mantle-core phase-change, no folded or thrusted mountains are to be expected, and this was duly confirmed by the detailed photography of the surface during the Mariner flypasts. If the current values for the mass and radius are substantially correct, the resulting curious constitution would have no relevance where the phase-change hypothesis is concerned. On the other hand it would certainly raise serious questions of a cosmogonical nature as to how so unusual a planet could have been formed.

As a result of the proximity of Mercury to the Sun and its smallness compared with other planets, the value of its mass as determined by dynamical means has had a long and chequered history of uncertainty. This goes back to Encke (1841) from a study of the motion of the short-period comet bearing his name, the orbit of which has fairly small inclination and perihelion-distance less than the semi-major axis of the orbit of Mercury. Authority for the value $(6000000)^{-1}$ of the solar mass, or 0.3315×10^{27}g, used by Rabe (1950, 1967) as starting-value for linear correction by the method of least-squares was ascribed to a paper by Stracke (1940), but no specific reference seems to be given therein for its adoption. The value can, however, be traced back to Newcomb (1895), and reveals some curious circumstances. After extensive investigations using all available observations of Venus, over 60,000 in number up to about 1891, with adjustments leading to solutions of increasing accuracy, Newcomb finally arrived at a value $(1 \pm 0.26)(8,400,000)^{-1}$ for the ratio of the mass of Mercury to that of the Sun with the mean-error range as shown. Then, strange to relate, without any stated explanation whatever, in setting down 'the best values' of the fundamental constants for the solar system as a whole, Newcomb suddenly took the extraordinary step of deciding to adopt the figure $(6,000,000)^{-1}$ as the definitive value for the mass, which was tantamount to making unnecessary almost if not the whole of the extensive investigation, for at the very outset of the study Newcomb states "the mass of Mercury which I have heretofore adopted, of $(7,500,000)^{-1}$, was rather a result of general estimate than of exact computation." Newcomb adds that in taking this value, of $(6,000,000)^{-1}$ he recognises that it is greater than any of the three mean-values arrived at en route by successive analyses of increasing refinement, "though not without (outside?) the range of easy possibility." In fact, the (reciprocal) mass-range implied by the mean-error factor $\pm$ 0.26 is from $(6,700,000)^{-1}$ to $(11,400,000)^{-1}$. This unaccountable decision to adopt seemingly quite arbitrarily a value not even within the mean-error range, when the original "general estimate" of $(7,500,000)^{-1}$ is, appears to be the ultimate source of the starting-values utilised in all modern investigations. The figure can have no more justification than if $(12,000,000)^{-1}$, lying just beyond the other extreme of the mean-error value, had been adopted as 'the best value'.

Prior to Newcomb, re-discussion by Backlund (1891) of the planetary perturbations of Encke's comet had led to a value of $(9,700,000)^{-1}$ for the Mercury-mass. Earlier still, von Asten (1872), again from analysis of the motion of comet-Encke, arrived at a value of $(7,600,000)^{-1}$. Both these values are seen to lie well within the mean-error range of the final result calculated by Newcomb, of $(8,400,000)^{-1}$.

Where solutions by least-squares from a great deal of observational data are concerned, the starting-value adopted for a particular quantity may be extremely crucial to the result obtained from it, especially when the values of a large number of variables are being sought, since all that the least-squares method can achieve is to determine a solution corresponding to the minimum sum of squares of residuals nearest to the starting-values, and if the value used at the outset for one of these should be considerably different from the true value, there might well be no possibility of the correction so emerging giving the right value, and it has always been the case in recent computations using radar time-delays and spacecraft signals that a great many variables are involved. As yet, solutions for the modern data from radar-ranging to planets (plus direct signals from the Vikings landed on Mars), and during flypasts of Mercury, seem not to have been made other than with a starting-value near to $(6,000,000)^{-1}$ for the mass, and it remains to be seen if any serious diminution of accuracy-of-fit, as measured by the sum of squares of residuals should result if the calculated Newcomb-value of $(8,400,000)^{-1}$, or the Backlund-value of $(9,700,000)^{-1}$, or even that calculated by von Asten of $(7,600,000)^{-1}$ were adopted.

REFERENCES AND NOTES

Anderson J.D. Astron.Journ. 73, S162, 1968.
Announcements of mass and radius of Venus from Mariner-V data.

Ash M.E., Kliore A., Melbourne W.G. et al., Science, 160, 985 et seq., 1968.
The radius of Venus as determined by radar methods.

Backlund J.O. Petrograd Memoirs, 1884, 1886, 1891-6.
For fuller reference to this work and that of von Asten see the obituary notice of Backlund in Mon.Not.Roy.Astron.Soc.76, 310, 1917.

Encke J.F. Astron. Nachrichten, 443, 1841.

Lyttleton R.A. On the Internal Structures of Mercury and Venus, Astrophys. & Space Science, 5, 18, 1969.

Lyttleton R.A. On the Internal Structure of Mars, Mon. Not.Roy.Astron.Soc., 129, 21, 1965.
Absence of folded and thrust mountains and of any magnetic field predicted, and possibility of rifting at surface.

Newcomb S. The Four Inner Planets and the Fundamental Constants of Astronomy, Washington, 1895.

Pettengill G.H. et al. Pioneer Venus Radar Mapping, Science 203, 806; and 205, 91, 1979.
These are first reports of measures of surface-topography of Venus from Pioneer-Orbiting Satellite.

Rabe E. Astron. Journ. 55, 112, 1950.
This describes the determination of the mass of Mercury (and other planets) based on observations of the minor planet Eros.

Rabe E. & Francis M.P. Astron.Journ. 72, 316 and 862, 1967.
These announce the discovery of a major conceptual error in Rabe's 1950 paper which when corrected led to the conclusion that the mass of Mercury became practically indeterminate from the Eros observations.

Stracke G. Abh.Preuss.Akad.Wiss. 1940, Math.-Naturwiss. Kl. No.7, 1940.

The value $(6,000,000)^{-1}$ solar mass for Mercury, hitherto taken as $(9,000,000)^{-1}$, used without stating source, but quoted as authority by Rabe (1950).

Wildt R. The Constitution of the Planets, Mon.Not.Roy. Astron.Soc. 107, 84, 1947.

9

Is the Constant of Gravitation Constant?

For the past forty years a ghost has been haunting the solar system, if not indeed the universe generally. Its apparition seems first to have been perceived dimly and announced by Dirac (1938), and has led to the notion that the constant of gravitation G may be changing with time. The idea emerged not on any strict theoretical basis but from considerations of a general nature arising from the existence of the large dimensionless numbers ($\sim 10^{39}$, 10^{78}) that can be constructed from known constants in physics and astronomy, and which show highly remarkable coincidences in their values. The whole matter has received extensive discussion, and there is a widespread strong belief that the coincidences have some deep theoretical significance. Studies of the problem have led to formulations by Dirac, Jordan, Brans & Dicke, and others of cosmologies differing from that based on standard general theory of relativity. This latter theory requires the constant of gravitation G to be an absolute constant, whereas in the proposed alternative theories G varies with the epoch.

If such were the case, additional factors would enter the theory of the foregoing chapters, which discuss the evolution of the Earth and its rotation, and the evolution of the lunar orbit, on the basis that G is constant. For the purpose of investigating these factors, it is not necessary here to give any detailed account of the cosmologies themselves, but merely to suppose that G is time-dependent. On the other hand, it is clearly of high importance to decide between the theories, and if a changing G is involved the validity of any such theory can only be settled by actual measurements aimed at testing predictions made by the theory. The theories themselves show that measures of the necessary precision appear at present to be possible only from dynamical motions within the solar system, and even with some of these difficulties are involved hindering attainment of the levels of accuracy required. The Einstein form of general relativity has survived all feasible experimental tests to date, thereby rendering extremely probable the a-priori case for G being a fundamental constant of invariable nature. Nevertheless it is of great scientific importance, if only as yet another possible test of that theory, for the consequences of a varying G to be studied observationally.

As earlier explained, it was gradually recognised that the rotation of the Earth undergoes intricate variations of such a nature as no longer to provide a reliable time-standard adequate to meet modern demands. This led to the introduction in about 1960 of so-called ephemeris-time based on the length of the tropical year for 1900. But if G is changing with time, and if $\dot{G}/G$ were negative, for example, as most of the new cosmological theories suggest, then all distances between the centres-of-gravity of objects in the solar system, such as the (osculating) semi-major axis <u>a</u> of a planetary orbit would be <u>increasing</u> systematically at a given rate given by $\dot{a}/a = -\dot{G}/G$, while the period of the orbit P would also be increased in accordance with $\dot{P}/P = -2\dot{G}/G$. Accordingly, if G is in fact changing, then ephemeris-time itself, since it is measured by means of a planetary orbit, would no longer correspond to true dynamical time. To meet this possibility, <u>atomic time</u> has been introduced, a time-rate based on resonant oscillations of the caesium atom, and this is regarded as invariable and providing a true measure of dynamical time independent of G.

To see how a constant-of-gravitation varying at some specified rate would affect tidal-friction theory, the orbital angular momentum of the Earth-Moon system, which is unaffected by a change in G, is in the notation of Chap. 4

$$h = Mmc^2 n/(M + m), \qquad \text{....(1)}$$

while if Kepler's third law involves a time-varying G, then it will take the form

$$n^2 c^3 = G(t)\ (M + m). \qquad \text{....(2)}$$

The mechanical couple N acting on the Moon, with -N acting to retard the rotation of the Earth, is the time-derivative of (1) and thus

$$N = \frac{dh}{dt} = Mm(M + m)^{-1}\ (2c\dot{c}n + c^2\dot{n}) \qquad \text{....(3)}$$

wherin, from (2), $\dot{n}$ and $\dot{c}$ are related by

$$2\,\frac{\dot{n}}{n} + 3\,\frac{\dot{c}}{c} = \frac{\dot{G}}{G}\ . \qquad \text{....(4)}$$

Using this relation to eliminate $\dot{c}$ from (3) yields

$$\dot{n} = -\,\frac{3(M + m)}{Mmc^2}\,N + 2n\,\frac{\dot{G}}{G}\ . \qquad \text{....(5)}$$

This relation shows that the complete value of n would consist of the usual part resulting from the mechanical couple N and, if G is changing, an additional purely kinematic part equal to $2n\dot{G}/G$. Thus even if there were no tidal friction in the system, $\underline{n}$ would be decreasing if $\dot{G}$ were negative and increasing if $\dot{G} > 0$.

It will be convenient to denote the complete value of n by n_a, the suffix indicating that the position of the Moon is to be measured against atomic time. The term in (5) involving N gives the purely mechanical rate of change of n arising from the lunar tidal couple, and this will be denoted by $\dot{n}_t$. Thus (5) may be written

$$\dot{n}_a = \dot{n}_t + 2n\frac{\dot{G}}{G}, \qquad \ldots.(6)$$

If G is unchanging with time then $\dot{n}_a = \dot{n}_t$, but not otherwise. For the rate of change of the lunar distance, (4) and (5) combined give

$$\frac{\dot{c}}{c} = \frac{2(M+m)}{Mmc^2 n} N - \frac{\dot{G}}{G}, \qquad \ldots.(7)$$

which shows that the lunar distance would increase both as a result of a positive tidal couple and a decreasing value of G.

Where the Sun is concerned, there will be a similar pair of equations to (5) and (7) which in the notation of Ch. IV now take the form

$$\dot{n}'_a = -\frac{3(m'+M+m)}{m'(M+m)c'^2} N' + 2n'\frac{\dot{G}}{G}, \qquad \ldots.(8)$$

the suffix again indicating measures against atomic time and

$$\frac{\dot{c}'}{c'} = \frac{2(m'+M+m)}{m'(M+m)c'^2 n'} N' - \frac{\dot{G}}{G}. \qquad \ldots.(9)$$

The angular velocity of the Earth ω will be changing as a result of the tidal couples $-N$ and $-N'$ acting on the planet, and ω will also change if the moment-of-inertia C is changing. A changing moment-of-inertia would occur from purely geophysical effects with G itself constant, as already seen in Chap. 6, or it would occur as a consequence solely of a changing G, for then gravity and the degree of compression caused by this would be altering ; and C could obviously alter through both sources in combination. However, details of the causes may be seen not to be relevant where derivation of the appropriate expressions for the apparent secular accelerations ν and ν' is concerned, but will be taken up later in this Chapter. For all cases, the rate of change of rotatory angular momentum of the Earth, as has been seen in Chap. 4 is given by

$$\frac{d}{dt}(C\omega) = -N - N' \qquad \ldots.(10)$$

or

$$C\frac{d\omega}{dt} = -N - N' - \dot{C}\omega \;. \qquad \ldots.(11)$$

Thus equation (15) of Ch. 4 is now replaced by

$$\nu = \dot{n}_a - \frac{n}{\omega}\dot{\omega}$$

$$= \frac{M+m}{Mmc^2}\left\{(\kappa-3)N + \kappa N'\right\} + n\frac{\dot{C}}{C} + 2n\frac{\dot{G}}{G}\;, \qquad \ldots.(12)$$

wherein as before $\kappa = Mmc^2 n(M+m)^{-1}(C\omega)^{-1}$ is the ratio of the orbital angular momentum of the Earth-Moon system to the rotatory momentum $C\omega$ of the Earth. For the Sun, the corresponding relation is

$$\nu' = \dot{n}'_a - \frac{n'}{\omega}\dot{\omega}$$

$$= -\frac{3(m'+M+m)}{m'(M+m)c'^2}N' + n'\frac{\dot{C}}{C} + \frac{n'}{C\omega}(N+N') + 2n'\frac{\dot{G}}{G} \quad ..(13)$$

But as seen in Chap.4., the first term on the righthand side in N' is in any case only of order 10^{-7} of the subsequent term in N' and so may be omitted as far below error-level, showing by (8) that n'_a could be sensibly different from zero only if G were changing. The equation for the solar apparent acceleration thus reduces to

$$\nu' = \frac{M+m}{Mmc^2}(\kappa N + \kappa N')\frac{n}{n'} + n'\frac{\dot{C}}{C} + 2n'\frac{\dot{G}}{G} \qquad \ldots.(14)$$

These equations (12) and (14) differ from (15) and (16) of Ch. 4 by the extra terms in $\dot{G}/G$ and of course reduce to them if $\dot{G}$ is put equal to zero.

Upon multiplying them through by $C\omega/n$ and $C\omega/n'$ in turn, and then using the values of ν and ν' (Ch. 4,p.72) converted to c.g.s. units, they become

$$(1 - 3/\kappa)N + (N' + \dot{C}\omega + 2C\omega\dot{G}/G) = (1.298 \pm 0.037 \times 10^{23} \quad \ldots.(15)$$

and

$$N + (N' + \dot{C}\omega + 2C\omega\dot{G}/G = (4.214 \pm 0.229) \times 10^{23} \quad \ldots.(16)$$

It may be noted as of special interest that these equations are again effectively in only two quantities, namely the lunar couple N, and the sum now of the three terms $N' + \dot{C}\omega + 2C\omega\dot{G}/G$. Remarkably enough therefore, the lunar couple N can itself be determined directly from the apparent secular accelerations ν and ν' even if either C or G or both should be changing with time : that is, the lunar couple comes out <u>clean</u> despite other complications. On the other hand, the solar couple N' obviously cannot be found at this stage, and to achieve this further considerations must again be introduced to settle the values of $\dot{C}$ and $\dot{G}/G$. By solving (15) and (16), the value of N is readily found as before to be

$$N = (4.74 \pm 0.38) \times 10^{23} \text{ c.g.s units.} \quad \ldots.(17)$$

The corresponding value of $\dot{n}_t$ then follows by means of (5) and (6) as

$$\dot{n}_t = (-27.2 \pm 2.2)'' \text{ cy}^{-2} . \quad \ldots.(18)$$

As seen earlier for the case of constant G, the time past when the lunar distance would have been comparable with the Earth-radius is only about 1.5×10^9 years ago. The difficulty of time-scale thereby arising would only be accentuated if G were decreasing with time, for it is seen from (7) that the term $-\dot{G}/G$ would be positive, augmenting the effect of the lunar couple and shortening the foregoing time. If however $\dot{G}/G$ were positive, it would have to be as large as $10^{-10}yr^{-1}$ to nullify the effect of N, and no cosmology has suggested a value as great as this.

Completing the solution of (14) and (15), they also yield

$$N'(\text{total}) + \dot{C}\omega + 2C\omega\dot{G}/G = (-0.52 \pm 0.44) \times 10^{23} \quad \text{....(19)}$$

The error-ranges given in (17) and (19) are formal standard errors based on the general assumption that the errors of ν and ν' are independent, though this could well not be entirely the case. As seen earlier in Ch. 4, the solar couple is known to consist of two parts : first a tidal-friction portion arising from the seas, oceans and body of the Earth that acts to retard the angular velocity, and second a smaller couple arising from thermal pressure produced by the atmosphere accelerative in its effect on the rotation. The value of this couple N'(thermal) is given by -0.37×10^{23} cgs units, as already noted in Chap. 4 p.79.

If a definite value is now adopted for $\dot{G}/G$, as for example that given by the cosmology of Brans and Dicke namely $\dot{G}/G = -3 \times 10^{-11}yr^{-1}$, then it follows at once from (6) that

$$\dot{n}_a = (-37.6 \pm 2.2)'' \text{ cy}^{-2}, \quad \text{....(20)}$$

and for this value of $\dot{G}/G$ it is also found that $2C\omega\dot{G}/G$ is -1.115×10^{23} cgs. As seen in Chap. 4 p.75, the solar tidal couple, N'(tidal), can as before be found from N given by (17) by simply scaling for linear friction, and this yields N'(tidal) = $(0.998 \pm 0.080) \times 10^{23}$ cgs. For quadratic friction, the scaling factor is different and yields N'(tidal) = $(1.246 \pm 0.099) \times 10^{23}$ cgs. Thus (19) yields for the two cases

$$\dot{C}\omega = (0.045 \pm 0.45) \times 10^{23} \text{ for linear friction}$$

and ....(21)

$$\dot{C}\omega = (-0.203 \pm 0.45) \times 10^{23} \text{ for quadratic friction.}$$

Since $\dot{C}\omega = -C\dot{\omega}_i$, these results are readily found to be equivalent to

$$\dot{\omega}_i/\omega = (-0.24 \pm 2.42) \times 10^{-11}\text{yr}^{-1} \quad \text{linear}$$

and ....(22)

$$\dot{\omega}_i/\omega = (+1.09 \pm 2.42) \times 10^{-11}\text{yr}^{-1} \quad \text{quadratic.}$$

As mentioned above, in addition to its purely kinematic effect, a reducing G would mean that the forces of compression within the Earth would be systematically decreasing too, and were this the sole factor involved it would obviously cause the planet to expand. So also in any case (G changing or not) does the slight effect of radioactive heating in causing the level of the base of the outer-shell to deepen, as already seen. Calculations show, however, that for any yet-proposed value of $\dot{G}/G$ these two sources of expansion even in sum are outweighed in the opposite sense by the conversion of mantle-material to the liquid-core phase as a result of radioactive heating. The following Table shows the calculated values of $\dot{\omega}_i/\omega$ for the present assumed value of $\dot{G}/G = -3 \times 10^{-11}\,\text{yr}^{-1}$, with the instant of collapse assumed to have occurred at the listed values of τ years ago, for both 3-zone and 2-zone models of the Earth. (The two sets of values again demonstrate how slight is the effect of the Bernal phase-change at the outer boundary of the mantle in the 3-zone case, which boundary is of course not present in 2-zone models.)

TABLE 20

$\dot{G}/G = -3 \times 10^{-11} yr^{-1}$

$(10^9$ yr)	3-zone models $\dot{\omega}_i/\omega$ $(10^{-11} yr^{-1})$	2-zone models $\dot{\omega}_i/\omega$ $(10^{-11} yr^{-1})$
- 2.5	5.18	5.35
- 3.0	4.37	4.51
- 3.5	3.79	3.92
- 4.0	3.37	3.48
- 4.5	3.05	3.15

It is plain that there is little agreement of either of the values of (22) for the two types of friction with any of those of the above Table. However, since the standard errors in (22) are larger in magnitude than the values themselves, some appearance of equality could always be achieved if an error sufficiently large and positive were regarded as being involved. Thus for quadratic friction, an error of the magnitude of the standard-error could bring $\dot{\omega}_i/\omega$ up to $3.51 \times 10^{-11} yr^{-1}$, which would correspond to $\tau = - 3.8 \times 10^9$yr on the 3-zone models, and $\tau = -3.9 \times 10^9$yr on 2-zone models. However, for linear friction it would be necessary to suppose a positive error of 1.34 times the standard error to bring the value of $\dot{\omega}_i/\omega$ up to even the least of those of the above Table.

The general conclusion emerges that a value of $\dot{G}/G = -3 \times 10^{-11} yr^{-1}$ could be reconciled only very marginally with the modern improved values of ν and ν' (or indeed with the values relied on by de Sitter and Jeffreys, which are not in fact much different), and this is particularly so for linear friction. The situation in regard to quadratic friction is rather less unfavourable if the whole of the tidal dissipation is so generated, though would still require an assumption of error in the positive direction as large as the standard-error. Agreement could then just be reached if τ corresponds to at least as far back as 3×10^9 yrs, with $\dot{\omega}_i/\omega$ only slightly greater than 4×10^{-11} yr^{-1}. The poorness of fit in this case stands out more clearly if given in graphical form. Fig. 13 shows the linear relation between N'(tidal) and $\dot{\omega}_i/\omega$ for this value of $\dot{G}/G$, and the values of $\dot{\omega}_i/\omega$ for a series of values of τ, together with N' (linear) and N' (quadratic). In the corresponding diagram for constant G (Fig. 10, p.129), the degree of fit is remarkably good in contrast, the vertical lines for the τ-values crossing well within the parallelogram defined by the standard-errors associated with tidal theory, whereas now for $\dot{G}/G = -3 \times 10^{-11}$ yr^{-1} the parallelograms barely extend to the τ-values associated with $\dot{\omega}_i/\omega$ as calculated from purely geophysical considerations.

For a numerical value of $\dot{G}/G$ as large as -6×10^{-11}yr^{-1} which in magnitude is about the highest rate of change of G suggested by any cosmological theory, there is even greater difficulty in reconciling the tidal friction results with those based on geophysical theory. With $\dot{n}_t = (-27.2 \pm 2.2)''$ cy^{-2} as given by (18), Eqn (6) requires the rate of change of n against atomic time to be

$$\dot{n}_a = (-48.0 \pm 2.2)'' \text{ cy}^{-2} \qquad \ldots.(23)$$

The value of the term $2C\omega\dot{G}/G$ in (19) is now -2.23×10^{23} cgs, and the corresponding results to (21) and (22) are

$$C\dot{\omega} = (1.16 \pm 0.45) \times 10^{23} \text{ for linear friction}$$

and $\ldots.(24)$

$$C\dot{\omega} = (0.91 \pm 0.45) \times 10^{23} \text{ for quadratic friction.}$$

Since $C\dot{\omega} = -C\dot{\omega}_i$, these are equivalent respectively to

$$\dot{\omega}_i/\omega = (-6.24 \pm 2.41) \times 10^{-11} \text{ yr}^{-1}, \qquad \ldots.(25)$$

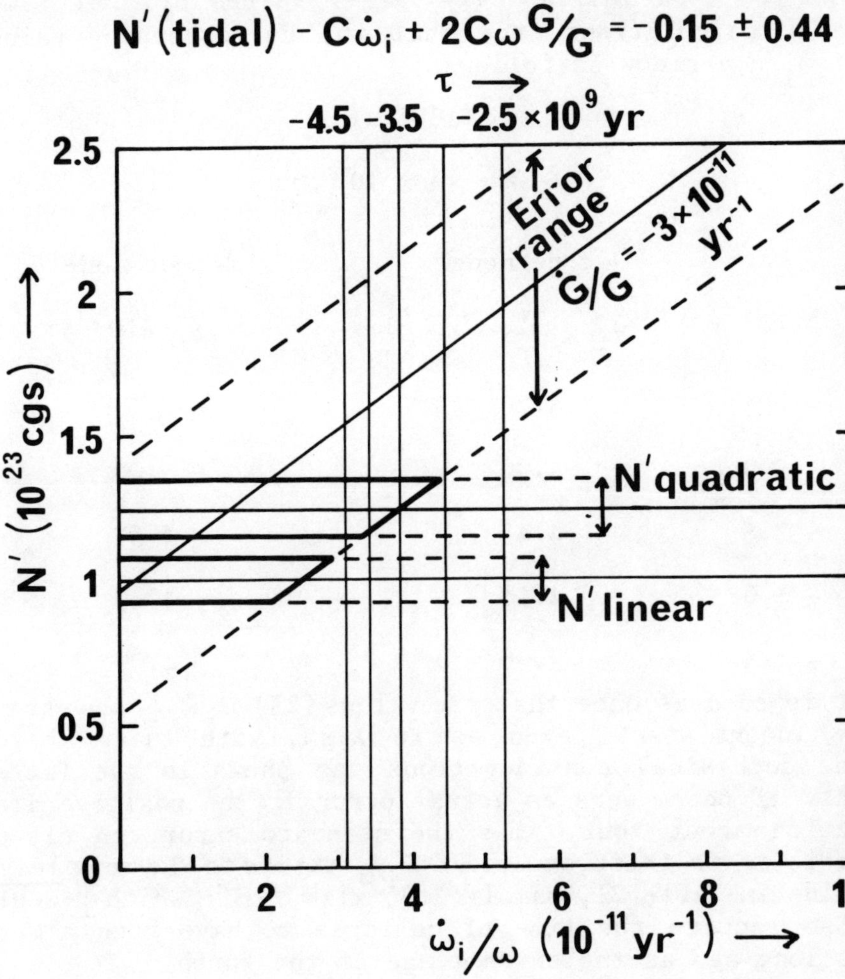
N′(tidal) − Cω̇ᵢ + 2Cω Ġ/G = −0.15 ± 0.44
τ →
−4.5 −3.5 −2.5 × 10⁹ yr
Error range
Ġ/G = −3×10⁻¹¹ yr⁻¹
N′ quadratic
N′ linear
N′ (10²³ cgs) →
ω̇ᵢ/ω (10⁻¹¹ yr⁻¹) →
2.5
2
1.5
1
0.5
0
2
4
6
8
10

Fig. 13

and ....(25)

$$\dot{\omega}_i/\omega = (-4.91 \pm 2.43) \times 10^{-11} \ yr^{-1}.$$

For the 3-zone and 2-zone models, making due allowance for the increasingly larger values of G at times past, calculations show that the corresponding values of $\dot{\omega}_i/\omega$ are now as follows :

TABLE 21

$\dot{G}/G = -6 \times 10^{-11} \ yr^{-1}$

	3-zone models	2-zone models
τ (10^9 yr)	$\dot{\omega}_i/\omega$ ($10^{-11}yr^{-1}$)	$\dot{\omega}_i/\omega$ ($10^{-11}yr^{-1}$)
- 2.5	5.60	5.79
- 3.0	4.90	5.06
- 3.5	4.45	4.58
- 4.0	4.14	4.27
- 4.5	3.96	4.07

It is seen at once that the values (25) of $\dot{\omega}_i/\omega$ are strongly inconsistent, even as to sign, with those based on geophysical considerations, as shown in the Table. Only if there were an actual error in the positive direction about four times the standard error, on either basis as to friction, could $\dot{\omega}_i/\omega$ attain to the very least value in Table 21, namely $3.96 \times 10^{-11}yr^{-1}$, which would also require the time of collapse to have been almost as long ago as the current age of the Earth.

To sum up : the conclusion emerges that the improved values of ν and ν' are most readily satisfied on the basis of constant G ; they can be weakly satisfied without going much beyond the error-range of $\dot{C}\omega$ for $\dot{G}/G = -3 \times 10^{-11} \ yr^{-1}$, but almost certainly cannot be satisfied for $\dot{G}/G = -6 \times 10^{-11} \ yr^{-1}$, or of course any numerically larger value.

If a decreasing G were the sole factor bringing about evolution of the Earth, the consequent gradual lowering of internal pressure would obviously lead to expansion of the planet, and as far as surface phenomena are concerned might cause rifting of the outer layers, but not the formation of mountains. When allowance is also made for geophysical causes, the amount of contraction would be expected to become less as the rate of decrease of G is increased from zero, but even for a value as large (numerically) as $\dot{G}/G = -6 \times 10^{-11} yr^{-1}$, the effects of the mantle-core phase-change dominate, and the overall contraction remains quite adequate in order of magnitude for all the mountain-building needed. In the following Table are shown the reduction in radius Δr_s, in surface-area ΔA, and in volume ΔV, as between the configuration immediately after collapse and the present radius, calculated for the case $\dot{G}/G = -3 \times 10^{-11} yr^{-1}$.

TABLE 22

$$\dot{G}/G = -3 \times 10^{-11} \text{ yr}^{-1}$$

$\tau(10^9$ yr)	Δr_s(km)	$\Delta A(10^6$ km^2)	$\Delta V(10^9$km^3)
- 2.5	260	43.6	138
- 3.0	253	41.3	134
- 3.5	246	40.1	130
- 4.0	239	38.9	126
- 4.5	231	37.7	122

Comparison with the values of Table 11, (Chap. 7, p.142) for G constant shows that, for the present value of $\dot{G}/G$, the various total changes are reduced by less than 10 per cent, and a volume of between 122×10^9 km^3 and 138×10^9 km^3 of rock to be redisposed during about twenty eras of orogeny, would remain quite ample in order of magnitude for the explanation of mountain-building. For the value $\dot{G}/G = -6 \times 10^{-11}\,yr^{-1}$, the reductions as would be expected are rather more, but are still of similar order of magnitude to the values for $\dot{G} = 0$. Thus, even if G should turn out not to be constant with time, but diminishing, it would not affect the success of the phase-change theory in accounting for the formation of mountains. Moreover, if G should turn out to be slightly positive, this acting alone would cause contraction by steadily increasing the pressures within the Earth, and thus in combination would augment contraction resulting from the phase-change effects.

Finally brief reference may be made to the present situation where measures of distances between the Earth and other bodies of the solar system have so far been made with a view to determining the possible variability of G. It has been seen that the increments in semi-major axis and period in a planetary orbit would be related to a change in G by

$$\Delta a/a = \tfrac{1}{2}\Delta P/P = -\Delta G/G. \qquad ....(26)$$

Since efforts are directed to determination of changes of distance over and above those occurring for purely dynamical reasons, it might appear at first sight, as Δa is proportional to a itself for given ΔG, that ranging from the Earth to other planets would be more effective in detecting changes than would be ranging to the Moon with its much smaller mean-distance. In practice, however, the situation turns out to be otherwise. Where time-delays of signals from Earth reflected by planets are concerned, a number of sources of error are found to enter. That the radar-signals must traverse the ionosphere and interplanetary plasma leads to some inaccuracy of measured travel-times, but the cratered and rugged topography of planets provides far from ideal reflecting surfaces, and much larger errors in this timing result from this cause, errors corresponding to distances of kilometric order.

The present situation has recently been reviewed by Stephenson (1980). Radar-ranging to the other terrestrial planets has now been conducted to an increasing extent during a period of more than a decade, but as yet the accuracy attained is far from adequate for any definite conclusion yet to be drawn concerning any variability of G, though further measures over a period of several years may well lead to an improvement of the position. Stephenson gives the following values for $\dot{G}/G$ that have emerged from the radar-data accumulated so far (1975) for the planets shown :

	$\dot{G}/G(10^{-11}yr^{-1})$	
Mercury	-6 ± 4	
Venus	-6 ± 6	....(27)
Mars	-25 ± 33	

Although these results are not inconsistent with $\dot{G} = 0$, it is also plain that no clear-cut conclusion on the question can be drawn from them at present. It is believed that with more observations the formal standard-error range may decrease at least as rapidly as the inverse-square of the time-span over which they are continued, but systematic error could well remain more difficult of detection.

Where actual ranging to the Moon is concerned, the available technique has proved much more successful, for the reason that so-called corner-reflectors have been placed on the actual lunar surface, 3 by means of Apollo-missions and 2 by means of Lunakhod-missions, and these have been continually used for measurements by laser-ranging from Earth. Surface topographical effects are eliminated, and an accuracy of distance from the source of light to the reflectors appears to be attainable within little more than 10cm as an average. The data accumulated so far over a period of 8 years since the first reflector was landed, have been analysed by a number of separate groups of workers. Thus, Williams et al.(1978) have determined a secular acceleration of mean-longitude given by

$$\dot{n} = (-23.8 \pm 4.0)'' \ cy^{-2},$$

corresponding to a rate of recession of the Moon from the

Earth given by

$$\dot{c} = (3.5 \pm 0.6) \text{ cm/yr}, \qquad \ldots.(28)$$

which may be compared with the value (4.02 ± 0.32)cm/yr implied by the lunar tidal couple N derived earlier from the ancient-eclipse data (Ch.4 p.74) on the basis of constant G. As far as the limits of their error-ranges are concerned, the two values are seen to overlap in the range (3.7 —4.1) cm/yr.

If G is changing, however, the actual value of $\dot{c}$ would differ from that based solely on the tidal couple and would include a portion of a kinematic nature resulting from $\dot{G}$ as given by equation (7), thus

$$\dot{c} = \frac{2(M + m)}{Mmcn} N - c\frac{\dot{G}}{G}, \qquad \ldots.(29)$$

For $\dot{G}/G = -3 \times 10^{-11}\text{yr}^{-1}$, the term $c\dot{G}/G$ is equal to -1.153 cm/yr, so that $\dot{c}$(total) = 5.18 cm/yr, a value in accord with (28) only if there were an actual error as large as about three times the standard-error. Similarly for $\dot{G}/G = -6 \times 10^{-11}\text{yr}^{-1}$, the total value of $\dot{c}$ would be 6.33 cm/yr which differs from (28) by about five times the standard-error. Again, the results to date are certainly not inconsistent with G being constant.

It is not the intention here to attempt a decision as to whether or not G differs significantly from zero, but only to set down for comparison the value of $\dot{c}$ as derived from direct measures of lunar-distance by laser ranging, with the value as determined from the ancient-eclipse data in terms of tidal-friction theory. It is considered by those involved in the ranging work that with continuing application of the laser-technique to a time-span T, the formal error-range can be expected to diminish roughly as $T^{-5/2}$. The data so far have covered a period of 8 years (to 1977), so if this expectation is realised the standard-error associated with the value (28) should become reduced to ± 0.1cm/yr after about another 8 years, but again it is not possible to say whether any systematic error may be involved, or what figure may by then replace the current value of (3.5 ± 0.6) cm/yr.

REFERENCES AND NOTES

Allen C.W. Astrophysical Quantities, 3rd edn, Athlone Press, 1973.

The definitions of the several time-standards and relations between them are given. It appears that the use of ephemeris-time instead of universal time was first suggested in 1948 by G.M. Clemence, and officially accepted at the 1958 I.A.U. meeting in Moscow, to come into general use by 1960.

Brans C. & Dicke R.H. Mach's Principle and Relativistic Gravitational Theory, Phys.Rev.124, 925, 1961.

Dirac P.A.M. A New Basis for Cosmology, Proc.Roy.Soc.A 165, 199, 1938.

Dirac P.A.M. On the Measurement of Cosmological Variations of G (1975 Conference). University of Florida Press, Gainsville, Fla., 1978. See also Proc.Roy. Soc.A 365, 19, 1979.

The latest form of the Dirac-theory predicts inward spiralling of the planets (see p.29 of the above paper).

Lyttleton R.A. & Fitch J.P. Effect of a Changing G on Moment-of-Inertia of Earth, Astrophys.Journ. 221, 412, 1978.

This paper shows that if G alone is changing (with no geophysical effects) the moment-of-inertia changes in accordance with $\dot{C}/C = -0.1724\dot{G}/G$. Allowance for the particular cosmology adopted can be made by including a numerical factor in the term in $\dot{G}/G$ in equations (4) and (26) above. In all cases it is close to unity and takes either sign according to the cosmology, but its presence would not seriously affect the position at present in view of the large error-ranges of (27).

Williams J.G, Sinclair W.S., & Yoder C.F. Geophys.Res. Letters 5(11), 943, 1978.

Index